Strategies to Navigate
the Four Stages
of Growth from
Start-up to Success

SMALL BUSINESS CEO

JENNY STILWELL

© Jenny Stilwell 2016
No reproduction without permission.
All rights reserved, including the right of production in whole or in part or in any form.
www.jennystilwell.com.au

National Library of Australia Cataloguing-in-Publication entry

Creator: Stilwell, Jenny, author.

Title: Small business CEO: strategies to navigate the four stages of growth from start-up to success/Jenny Stilwell.

ISBN: 9780994545213 (paperback)

Subjects: Small business – Management.

Small business – Growth.

Success in business.

Business planning.

Dewey Number: 658.022

DISCLAIMER: The similarity of any examples to actual businesses owned by people with the same names as those in this book is coincidental. The examples have been created to form fictional businesses with principles that would apply if those businesses actually existed. Names, companies and situational details have been created. Any real company examples either use information available in the public domain, or have been authorised for inclusion by the owner of the business. Other information related to client challenges and strategies throughout the book is presented in a general context. I am not a lawyer, accountant, or financial advisor and you should always consult these experts before acting on this information related to a change in your business finances.

Dedication

I dedicate this book to my family, for their lifelong support of my business and writing ambitions.

I dedicate it also to Bob Secombe,
who gave me my start.

Contents

Preface **vii**

Chapter 1: Making the Shift to CEO **1**
Chapter 2: Business Models and Scalability **13**
Chapter 3: Stage 1 – Foundation **27**
Chapter 4: Stage 1 Action Plan – Foundation **41**
Chapter 5: Stage 2 – Build Structure **99**
Chapter 6: Stage 2 Action Plan – Build Structure **113**
Chapter 7: Stage 3 – Business Expansion **143**
Chapter 8: Stage 3 Action Plan – Business Expansion **151**
Chapter 9: Stage 4 – Optimise Value **195**
Chapter 10: Stage 4 Action Plan – Optimise Value **209**
Chapter 11: Staying on Track **223**

Acknowledgements **229**
About Jenny Stilwell **231**
Other Resources **233**

Preface

I have always been a fan of the 'work smarter not harder' strategy. Unfortunately, I see so many small business owners working harder and harder to get the results they want, but they aren't working on the right things. Eventually a lot of them are forced to give up under the pressure of it all, and others become disillusioned about having their own business.

It isn't an easy journey and don't ever let anyone tell you that it is! But when you eventually get it right, it can be so rewarding and fulfilling.

Success in business – even small successes – can be so exciting, and in many ways make you feel that anything is possible. However, when you face challenges you don't know how to deal with, or find yourself in difficult circumstances where you have no reference points, what do you do? If you can't diagnose your own situation and problem, you can't move through it.

Small Business CEO is designed to give you the reference points you will need as the driver of your own business. My objective is to break down the entrepreneurial business journey into different stages, to help give you clarity and direction – and the right strategies – at each stage.

It's fair to say that I have been through all of the challenges and stages of growth first-hand, as my own journey has encompassed not only entrepreneurial ventures and the corporate world, but also CEO roles in both my own and others' companies. I have also advised hundreds of small-business owners through my consulting, programs and resources. So I bring to this book the structure and disciplines from the corporate world, and the trials and tribulations from the entrepreneurial world.

Small Business CEO will demonstrate that as a business grows from start-up through to a more substantial and complex entity, four key stages define growth. Parallel to the growth of the business, the owner must grow to become a CEO.

A growing and expanding business requires a strategic approach, and the people who will ultimately work in your business want a leader, not a micromanager. You need to shift your role from 'business owner' to 'CEO'. This may be a subtle shift, but it is a real one.

Small Business CEO takes an in-depth look at each of the four stages of growth, and the strategic approach you need to address the typical challenges. It does not cover everything regarding strategy or management for each stage. Having a focus on three strategies for each stage is easier to digest, manage and implement.

What follows each stage is an action plan for each strategy. This is a how-to guide with worksheets and templates that will further develop the professional skills of both new business owners and small business CEOs.

Before self-selecting and going to the stage where you think your business is, I recommend that you read the first chapter to be sure, and then go straight to your action plan.

You can then read about the stage you're in and recognise some of the challenges you face and what is behind them. You can also look ahead to the next stage of growth and be better prepared for when you reach it.

Alternatively, you can just read from start to finish, then go back to your stage of growth and action plan.

I know this structured four-stage approach will add value to your business as it has to mine and those of my clients, by helping you identify the strategic priorities that are most important to you right now.

Ultimately, it is my belief that the primary purpose of creating and growing a business should be to create a better life for yourself and those you love. Please don't become consumed by the 'better business' bit, and forget about the 'better life' you can create!

Better strategy, better business, better life.

Enjoy your journey!

CHAPTER 1

Making the Shift to CEO

BUILDING a successful business – and ultimately creating a better life in the process – is a bit like training to become an elite athlete.

You don't become a great swimmer without the hours of training. You will never play off scratch just because you have a natural golf swing. And you will never be able to complete a 100-kilometre bike race without enduring many hours building up stamina on your bike first.

In business, you need to put in the time and effort to hone your skills and improve your game. You learn as you go and do what it takes to become better and more capable, and you eventually progress from novice to master. You need enough stamina to run a marathon!

However, the thing with business building is that it becomes more and more complex as you continue to play it. When you start you will be intent on getting your name out there and getting new customers and clients. As you grow, you will need to shift your focus and energy into managing a team of people and a range of products and services, and looking after a lot more customers. You may have grown into having multiple departments in your company, and there will be way more financial and operational aspects to control.

With business growth comes professional and personal growth. How you handle your personal growth will be up to you, but this book aims to guide you through the shift you need to make in your professional development and skills.

You will most likely experience the four stages of growth as part of this development and improvement process.

In Australia, small businesses are typically defined as those having between three and 15 employees, with medium-sized enterprises employing up to 200 people.

These are sizeable companies, and whether you have a team of 15 or 115, they need direction and leadership if you are to grow. That means making the shift in how you think about your business, how you grow it and how you manage it.

The shift you need to make is from being the business owner to being the CEO of your business.

Let's get started.

CEO versus business owner

Differences in approach between a CEO and a business owner become evident at various stages of growth. Table 1.1 includes a summary of these differences. They may not mean much to you if you are currently in Stage 1, but will definitely become more important to your success as your business grows.

Table 1.1: Different approaches of a CEO and a business owner

CEO approach	Business owner approach
Have a capital-raising strategy	*Never* consider debt to fund growth
Set clear accountabilities for your team and let them do their jobs	Get involved in everything
Make your own position description clear to your management team	You don't need a job description – it's your company after all and you don't have to explain what you do to anyone
Employ people who are experienced and will *add value* to the business	Employ juniors because they cost less and they can be shaped to how you like to work
Make tough decisions and let people go when required	Fail to make tough decisions and let under-performers stay, while better employees leave
Form a clear vision for the business, which you articulate to the team	Fail to have any vision for the growth of the business; if you do have one, keep it to yourself
'Think' more than 'do'	'Do' more than 'think'
Focus on priorities	Focus on too many things at once that may not be priorities – 'bright shiny object syndrome'
Track performance against targets with a management dashboard	A management *what?*
Be a leader you would want to follow	Have a different set of rules for yourself
Leave the office and talk to/meet with other people in other businesses and industries, looking for ideas, innovation and new opportunities	Be at work all the time and mostly at your desk

CEO approach	Business owner approach
Develop frameworks and criteria and set expectations for performance	Change your mind frequently and expect everyone else to automatically course-correct
Always have the end-game in mind as it helps you make the right strategic decisions	What end-game?

Even with all these fundamental differences in approach, the primary difference I see is that business owners fail to evolve and up-level their own role. They want to be involved in everything, while employing relative juniors or other people who don't have the experience for what the business requires. The competency gap between the owner and the next level down is way too big. The owner still has to step in and make decisions and solve problems and give plenty of direction to their team, because the team lacks the skills and experience to take charge.

Many business owners lament the growth of their team for this reason – they say 'I don't know why I employ all these people when I have to do most of it myself.'

Finally, if you're really serious about wanting to grow your business, there are two big reasons you need to make the shift:

1. **You have to let go if you want to grow**

    You can't do it all, especially when your business becomes more complex. You can only utilise other people to help you grow when your own role changes.

    When you let go and step up, everything shifts and your perspective will naturally shift. You will see your business with fresh eyes.

2. **You need to be strategic about your business – and your role in it – if you want a better business and a better life**

    You need to shift how you think, and *think* more than *do*. Your team will do what needs to be done to enable the business to grow – you direct them. That's when you become a captain with a capable team, as opposed to a team with one too many players and no captain.

I will cover 'letting go' more under Stage 2, as this is the stage at which you must shift or implode. As you transition from Stage 1 into Stage 2, your business will have more people, more complexity, and greater need for clarity of direction, roles, performance and opportunities. We will go into 'being strategic' in Stage 3 – Business Expansion.

For now, use this book as a guide to take you through each of the four stages of business growth and what you need to focus on to navigate through them successfully. Use the tools provided to help you implement strategies and actions, and improve your skills as a leader as you go. You can use these tools whenever you need them and you can pass them onto members of your team to use as well. The better equipped your staff are, the more value they will add to your business.

> The primary difference I see is that business owners fail to evolve and up-level their own role.

So, you get the idea about making the shift. Are you a business owner or a CEO? I hope you have identified yourself as a CEO if you are serious about building your business, because you will only be able to build an asset or leave a legacy with that approach. Whether you want to build many offices around the globe with teams of people, or work from home with your team either spread around the globe or all in the office together, it doesn't matter. Whatever business model you choose is secondary to your approach.

The most successful CEOs always keep focused on the vision of where they are taking their business, but also focus on priorities in the present and immediate term that need to be addressed. Take deliberate steps today that will help you arrive at the point where you want to be tomorrow.

The 4 stages of growth

A business goes through many stages of growth during its life cycle. Because we don't always take the time – or have the time – to think about our businesses in a strategic way, we often make the mistake of adopting the wrong strategies and priorities at the wrong time. Understanding which stage your business is in, and what happens at that stage, will give you clarity straight away. You can then work on the necessary strategies and action plans for renewed business growth.

In running both my own and others' companies, I know from experience what it takes to navigate through them, as well as the obstacles and challenges that can derail you. I've advised hundreds of business owners in my role as strategic mentor, and as a result identified four key stages from inception through to sale.

The four stages are:

1. Foundation
2. Build Structure
3. Business Expansion
4. Optimise Value.

The stages are mostly sequential, but a business will often straddle two stages as the owner reaches for the next level of business growth, while still dealing with the demands of the current level. Occasionally a business may need to regroup and go back to the fundamentals of a previous stage. Unfortunately, we know that far too many enterprises crash and burn before reaching the exciting heights of a big payday when the owner sells and is finally rewarded for years of hard work.

And therein lies another reason for writing this book. Too many times I've seen people reach out for help, only to be overwhelmed by all the latest strategies for employing a team, lead generation, developing one-page business plans or killer websites, being more productive, selling and closing techniques, online marketing, building a brand, and so on. Many of these strategies are valuable, but the problem is that most people don't know what to focus on at what stage.

> Each stage of growth requires focus on different, and very specific, strategies. The business owner needs clarity on the *right* strategies to take their business through to its next stage.

It's perfectly natural to become overwhelmed when you have a problem and you're looking for a solution, but you don't know what sort of solution or information you need.

By simplifying business growth into these four primary stages, my aim is to guide you through what you need to focus on when you find yourself in a particular set of circumstances, and how to execute the appropriate strategy.

Here is a summary of the Four Stages of Growth. You'll find details in the following chapters.

Stage 1: Foundation

Typically, a Foundation business is run by an individual who may have some ad hoc or part-time help to perform certain roles. Many Foundation business owners are happy being in Foundation and have no desire to build a team or bigger overheads, and they like the job they've created for themselves.

Many service providers have Foundation businesses – consultants, physiotherapists, artists, tutors, plumbers and bookkeepers are all examples of individuals who provide service in an area of expertise and who *are* their businesses.

There is nothing wrong with deciding to stay in Foundation, but it relies heavily on one person to bring in new business, service the clients and manage the cash flow, plus manage any external support people. It takes a lot of discipline and focus to stay in Foundation as it's a constant cycle of acquiring and servicing clients – marketing, selling, servicing, relationship-building. Some Foundation businesses can continue to operate in this mode for 20, 30 or 40 years, if the owner wishes.

Another type of Foundation business is the one that struggles for survival. We all know the statistics about how many small businesses fail in the first or second year, and how many are still in existence five years later. The vast majority are in the Foundation stage.

What defines these businesses is their inability to reach a critical mass where they can survive. They don't develop their client base to a size that provides sustainable ongoing business. They haven't developed the best marketing strategies to bring in new business opportunities. They don't have the right support. The business owner is overwhelmed trying to do this, that and the other. These businesses become statistics. However, with the right guidance in the early stages of their existence, their results could have been different.

For those that succeed and want to continue to grow, the next stage is to build structure.

Stage 2: Build Structure

At this stage, the business now has more of everything – more clients, more work, more opportunities, more people, more income, more paperwork, more suppliers – more moving parts. Because of the 'more' factor, it needs systems, the right legal and organisational structures and a focus on building a cohesive team.

More than any other stage, this is where businesses can, and do, crash and burn, because the owner fails to focus on structure.

It is imperative at this stage for the owner to step up and run their business strategically with an eye on growing both the business and a team around them, rather than continuing to live in the moment and react to each day's challenges in isolation. This approach only results in more struggle and less fulfilment. It's an exciting stage but a potentially unstable and dangerous one.

Stage 3: Business Expansion

This can occur within a short period of time or after many years of incremental but ad hoc growth. Many small businesses set random targets like 'increase sales 10% next year', or 'increase the bottom line to 18%'.

So, a goal like 'increase sales by 10%' may mean they take on a private-label customer, which will actually result in 25% growth. However, this growth comes at a considerable cost: the increased headcount to handle this client, a possible increase in warehouse space and logistics overheads, and significantly reduced margin. There are not only the actual costs of increasing sales 25%, but the additional management time and resources required as a result, plus in most cases an increased level of stress and pressure on the business owner.

If this growth is the goal, there isn't a problem with the strategy. However, if the primary goal and focus of the company had been 'increase profit before tax by 18%', their strategic decision-making would have been different.

Business expansion requires considerable research, analysis and consideration of the organisation's values and priorities. What is really important to us? What do we want from business growth? Where will we invest our resources? What will our strategic focus be?

When companies get this strategic, they're in Stage 3 and being proactive about growth rather than reacting to incremental opportunities.

Stage 4: Optimise Value

At this stage, the owner is executing the strategies required in order to sell their company. Ideally, this will be a consideration in Stage 3 when strategies for expansion are being developed.

I have heard many business owners talk about maybe selling their business one day, and what they might do to make that happen, and what they would consider selling for. I have never heard anyone articulate the model they are emulating and the plan for expansion and subsequent sale.

It's a travesty to see someone work so hard to build a business most of their life, only to be under-rewarded when they sell. This happens because they don't know what to focus on to prepare for sale and what acquirers would consider as the real value in the business, and they fail to get professional advice to facilitate the sale and negotiation process.

Seasoned businesspeople – who have been through recessions, crises, and challenges that would test anyone – frequently stumble at this vital stage because they can see the finish line and bolt before consulting the experts. Please don't let this be you! Dive into the strategies for Stage 4 and be well prepared in advance.

Hybrid stages

It is not uncommon to find your business straddling two stages. For example, you are in Stage 2 and need to build more structure into your business to take some of the load away from your own shoulders. At the same time you are faced with some great opportunities for expansion. You need to get your house in order first so you are set up to take advantage of the opportunities presenting themselves.

If you don't have strong foundations, you won't be able to support the added weight of a heavier structure. If you don't address the structure, your business won't be able to support further expansion. If you don't have a track record of strategic business growth, it will be more difficult to optimise the potential value of your business. In general, the earlier stage will be more of a priority than the next.

Business growth is not always neatly sequential. Problems and disruptions occur that need to be dealt with at all stages of growth, and these often don't have clear paths for resolution.

The most common hybrid stage for established businesses is to juggle the need to focus on growth and building structure. In this case, your action plan will be a combination of things from all the relevant strategies throughout this book. If you're in a hybrid stage, you can create your own hybrid action plan from the four stages.

Now you know where you are, you can dive into the appropriate chapter to get clarity on your strategy.

Chapter highlights

- The fundamental difference between a CEO and a business owner is a focus on growth: the CEO spends more time on thinking and strategy away from the office, whereas the business owner is at their desk, more focused on the doing.

- CEOs realise the importance of employing experienced people to add value to their team. Knowing they have to pay well to get top talent, they consider it an important investment in their business. Business owners fear the cost of such people, favouring inexperience instead.

- To shift from business owner to CEO, you need to start thinking strategically and let your team step up as you step back from the coalface to start driving the business.

- Business longevity is not an indicator of what stage you are in.

- The four stages:

    Foundation – from start-up to becoming profitable with a stable client base.

    Build Structure – building a team and implementing systems to phase yourself out of the day-to-day detail.

    Business Expansion – growing beyond your current team and marketplace into new territory, be it product, service or market.

    Optimise Value – your exit from the business.

CHAPTER 2

Business Models and Scalability

It is important to consider business models and scalability before we dive into specific strategies and action plans.

As a small business, you need to give considerable thought to what business model (or combination of models) you will use to scale up your business to have more reach and more profit.

A business is said to be scalable when it can be operated on a much bigger scale – more products can be developed, more goods can be manufactured, more services can be delivered, more distribution channels can be utilised, more customers can be reached: that is, more volume, more sales, more customers, more reach, more profit.

The key is more profit.

To get it right, it's crucial to understand how the most common business models operate.

Business models

There are risks and rewards in all models. Here is an overview.

Online business

This model is appealing to many people who think they can create passive income via an online business.

Building a purely online business requires significant capital to invest in two things: marketing and a sound online business infrastructure. While the margin on digital products is virtually 100%, the cost of supporting and marketing this model with tangible products that need development, warehousing and distribution is high.

A website is fine to showcase your products, but you need volume if you want to make a living from it. Volume comes from massive marketing activity. Volume sales require a robust ecommerce site supported by an efficient back-end warehouse system. If you plan to sell products online and lots of them, they need to be stored somewhere and they need to be picked and packed and sent to the right customers. You need a returns policy and a system to process returned products. You also need a back-end system to move slow-selling and discontinued stock. Search YouTube for a video on how Amazon handles all its back-end logistics to get another perspective for this massive online business.

If your product is intangible, such as digital products (audio, video, downloads), you will be able to build an online business if you have a polished and practised marketing system. This marketing system will need to balance giving away free content in order to build followers, with strategies to convert leads to sales. These strategies include complex and precise online marketing campaigns backed up by affiliate programs, auto-responder sequences that sit behind your campaigns, and using social media as another channel to market to build your pipeline. There is an art to this and if you want to base your whole business model on it, you will need a team of web-savvy marketers, a host of technology and possibly content creators to support you.

All of the purely online businesses that I have seen, started by business owners wanting to generate passive income, fail to support the owner. They have all needed to be supplemented by an additional income stream and/or a bricks-and-mortar presence in the market.

While the margin on digital products is virtually 100%, the cost of supporting and marketing this model with tangible products that need development, warehousing and distribution is high.

It is a great model to combine with your business, rather than have as your only source of income.

Notonthehighstreet.com

This UK-based organisation is an online 'emporium' – bigger than a shop – for small product-based businesses. It provides all the marketing and PR to drive traffic to its site, and once its online 'retailers' sell a product, they receive a commission. It also receives income in terms of online lease payments from its online tenants. Revenues have grown to double-digit millions of pounds sterling.

The results have been outstanding, but the business has been built on massive marketing and PR efforts and advertising costs. The website would take specialist resources to maintain, update and channel through to its social media sites.

Service business model

Many small businesses are set up by people who have skills and knowledge that their clients will pay for. It is typically easier and faster to set up a service business than a product-based one.

Sole practitioner

Consultants, health practitioners, bookkeepers and the like have the challenge of adding people who are capable of delivering the same or similar standard of service as they do. They can scale their business by 'cloning' themselves. However, if they enjoy being a sole practitioner, their income will be capped unless they find other ways to generate revenue. The other common challenge with this business model is to be paid for what you know or can do, before you give it away for nothing. Ideas, plans, strategies and designs all fall into this category.

One of the best ways to increase your income with this traditional model is to convert your core methodologies or expertise into intellectual property. For example, an artist – let's say a painter – can create original canvases, which are then converted to prints of different sizes, framed and unframed; their art can become gift cards; it can become printed fabric, which in turn can be converted into products, and so on.

Consultants can use their own proprietary methodology to create solutions for clients. This can be delivered one-on-one as a 'done for you' service, as a workshop so clients can do it themselves, as a series of information products, or as a seminar to teach other consultants how to do the same thing.

If you can convert your service offering into other media and delivery channels, you have the opportunity to extend your income and grow without needing to add more people to your business.

Service business within a business

Many recruiters and real estate agents, and some consulting firms, fit this model. If the company has a well-established name in the market, it is relatively easy to employ more recruiters, real estate agents or consultants who leverage off the goodwill or brand recognition of the organisation. They can hire their own support teams, bring clients with them into the new company, and build their own client base under the umbrella of the organisation they work for.

They're not paid a fully loaded salary like in a traditional firm; most companies pay a small base with the remainder as a commission based on the percentage of business that person brings into the company.

This model enables these sorts of service businesses to grow quickly. However, just as these service practitioners can come in and be operational very quickly, they all have their own way of working. In the absence of sound processes and systems, a business that grows very quickly in this way can become disconnected and unmanageable. These service practitioners can also leave just as quickly and if they're good, their clients will leave the firm and follow them instead.

Information marketing model

The model here is to create something once and repurpose it. That is, create your IP and turn it into many different forms to deliver in many different ways. Instead of providing a one-on-one service, this repackaging of your IP will enable you to provide value in a one-to-many model.

In one of my consulting companies, I worked with clients one-on-one to improve their businesses and help them grow. I could only work with so many clients at once, and while I charged well for the value I delivered, my income was capped using this strategy.

Additionally, I then started to deliver the same value to groups of clients in a CEO mastermind group. This was membership-based and enabled me to work with several clients at once.

Then I developed information products, which didn't produce money while I slept because they still required a lot of marketing campaigns to promote them. I didn't have that marketing integrated into an automated system, but it *was* another income stream.

There are plenty of experts on this topic who are making bazillions with information marketing empires. Whether you make millions or thousands, information marketing is a viable model (or addition to your existing service model) for even the smallest business to add another revenue stream.

If you can deliver your expertise to your clients in person, you can also do it via many other forms: teleseminars, webinars, MP3s, videos, PDFs, workbooks, email courses, apps, books, workshops, speaking, conferences and any combination of these. Crafting your content and repackaging it will enable you to reach different delivery channels and market segments.

Licensing and franchising

The Rip Curl case study on page 24 is an innovative licensing model. More common forms of licensing are for software and accreditation to use others' systems, methodologies, branding and business models.

Well-known examples that you have probably had some contact with in your business life are numerous profiling tools such as Myers Briggs (MBTI®), DiSC® and StrengthsFinder that are licensed to accredited professionals to use with their clients. Anyone can do these tests online, but if you want to be able to train others and run workshops and use their tools, you need to be accredited by the parent company.

Companies like E-Myth and ActionCOACH train consultants, coaches and others worldwide in order to accredit them to use their packaged methodologies. People pay for the accreditation training, which entitles them to operate under the brand of these sorts of companies. ActionCOACH now is a franchise model.

Franchising is also a great business model if you own the IP and are selling franchises to others to enable them to use your IP. If you've done your research and you like the idea of franchising, you need to be excellent at systemising your business so it can be duplicated and run by others. A general rule is that if a business is duplicated at least three times (for example a dog grooming service in three locations or a fast food store opened in three different areas) with successful results, you may have a model that could be set up as a franchise.

You receive not only the sale price when you sell a franchise, but also ongoing royalties and a contribution to the marketing budget from each franchisee annually.

On the flip side, considerable research is required into the market potential for your particular business, as well as a considerable investment in legal and financial resources to set it up. And don't forget the 'proof of concept' for the potential return on investment.

Retail model

Online shopping is rising as a preferred way to shop by some segments of the market. Increasing imports offering low-cost alternatives make 'Australian made' an expensive option for the price-conscious shopper. Bricks-and-mortar retail stores often struggle to compete, and are more often than not constrained by margins and cash flow. However, I believe there is a demand and a place for niche retailers, those who provide an experience for their customers, and those who build a portfolio of mixed products, services and delivery methods.

Retailers who don't believe in marketing or innovation will not be here for the long term. In order to survive and thrive, retailers also need to be mindful of their sales per square metre and how much more yield they could generate from new products and new service offerings. Compare these two local businesses:

RETAIL MODEL: CASE STUDY 1

A small bakery had been serving local customers for years. It refused to innovate. The owners gave every reason why they couldn't offer pre-made sandwiches, rolls and wraps for their customers, even though customers had been asking them to for years. When they finally started selling coffee, it was the 'old' way, with plastic cups and appalling instant coffee! The owner explained that it was 'cheap and perfect for the tradies'. Trouble was, all the tradies like real coffee. A new owner has taken over and quickly revitalised this local business, offering customers what they actually want – including real coffee – and is constantly thinking of new ideas to introduce.

RETAIL MODEL: CASE STUDY 2

A restaurant I know started out 20 years ago as a tiny cafe. The space next door became available and they leased that too. Fast forward to the present and they've turned their two retail spaces into a large cafe and restaurant (open daily plus Thursday through Saturday for dinner), a deli with an amazing selection of produce and take-home meals, a burger bar set up as a 'hole in the wall' at the back of the restaurant in the side street, an ice-cream window adjacent to the burger bar, and a catering company. In addition, they host masterclasses with well-known local chefs several times a year, and you can hire the restaurant for the evening if you want to have a celebration or private event on the evenings they aren't open for dinner. They also took over the Japanese cafe next door. They retained the Japanese owner but rebranded the space and did a new fitout, to become a more upmarket and contemporary Japanese takeaway store.

There are many more examples where people combine services with retail into innovative experiences for their customers. This combination of products, services and a little bit of theatre is what keeps retail alive as a viable business model.

Some examples of retail businesses are included in Chapter 4 (Foundation).

Branded retail chain

In 2007, the *Sydney Morning Herald* reported that the local handbag and accessory company Mimco sold for somewhere between

$40 million and $50 million to a private equity company wanting to build a portfolio of speciality retail brands.

Globally, a handful of companies own most of the world's luxury brands. For example, LVMH has acquired a portfolio of luxury brands including Louis Vuitton, Tag Heuer, Bulgari, Dior and many more. Locally, private equity companies are starting to show a similar pattern.

Investors saw value in Mimco in the high-margin product, the opportunity to expand from 17 Mimco stores, opening another 10 each year, plus the potential for considerable product extension. The brand had national exposure and recognition with its own branded stores as well as being sold in 34 David Jones stores. Now, Mimco is owned by South African retail group, Woolworths Holdings Limited, and is part of their sizeable stable of brands.

Another example of this model is kikki-K, the home office products specialist retailer. The founder, Kristina Karlsson, started with one retail store and a website. She has systematically grown her company into a national network of stores with an international presence. She combined online sales with the retail footprint, with the online store growing into what is effectively the 'largest' in terms of sales (she shared this at an event a few years ago so it may have changed now).

Building a brand sold by other retailers (private label)

This business model is based on picking up distribution rights for other brands, licensing agreements to create new products (such as Disney-branded children's bath products), or creating private-label products for supermarkets and national retailers. This is an increasingly dangerous model. Major retailers can make these companies redundant by going directly to supply and development teams in low-cost-base countries like China, where they can develop and manufacture their own products without any third-party intervention. Or they can have private-label products manufactured by local companies without the need for any middleman.

In addition, brand companies are frequently put in the position of developing home-brand products for the national retailers that will effectively compete against their own brands on the shelf. The three-tiered home-brand strategy of good, better, best positioning and pricepoints has been making it increasingly difficult for independent brands to compete in the national retail environment, particularly in supermarkets.

These brand-development companies will have limited value compared to the companies that build their own brands.

Manufacturing model

In the manufacturing model, you typically make products for other people, rather than owning your manufacturing as a vertically integrated brand organisation.

As you expect, in the age of cheap imports and accessible low-cost production in other countries, manufacturing is a shrinking industry in Australia. We have such high costs of living it is difficult for manufacturing to be sustainable. However, there are niche manufacturers who apply innovation, design and technology to their production process, resulting in a quality Australian-made product that cannot be copied by cheap alternatives.

For the most part though, small manufacturers are impacted by low buying power and relegated to higher prices from suppliers, whether those suppliers are local or offshore.

Their customers, many of whom make brands to be sold into national retailers, are being squeezed down on price and margin by these retailers. As a result, the end of the chain is the manufacturer who can only haggle over a few cents in a tightly controlled supply chain process dictated by the retailers.

National retailers and supermarkets are demanding massive margins – upward of 70% – leaving the supplier to negotiate down on every single element in their supply chain.

Local manufacturers need to have a sales and marketing-driven customer focus, in order to be innovative and proactive in the development cycle. They need to have a strong value proposition and a point of difference over lower-cost alternatives. They would also benefit from their own offshore sourcing partners and suppliers, and the creation of their own brand stories to add more value to their customers.

Any business owner benefits from going out into the world and looking at other models and industries in different markets, and adding value by bringing some of those ideas to their own market and customer base.

Scalability

One of the most profitable ways for small businesses to scale up is to develop intellectual property (IP) such as technology for automation, software and apps, licensing, methodologies and processes.

It's also important to know that there are traps inherent in scaling up that you need to carefully navigate. Most businesses scale up organically. Occasionally businesses get capital injections to take them skyrocketing from zero to millions. Other businesses scale up too fast; they lose control, crash and burn.

BOBBI BROWN COSMETICS

Family was always Bobbi Brown's priority. She didn't want to keep travelling as it meant being away from her three children for too long.

Bobbi started out creating new cosmetic products, working with one development chemist. Her first major sale was into Bergdorf Goodman and then other major retailers wanted to stock her products.

Estee Lauder's son Leonard offered to buy her business because he had all the resources to scale it up. He had an army of development chemists and global distribution channels. Bobbi knew that she couldn't scale up with one chemist, but she did want to keep growing her brand. So she sold in 1995 and has been the COO of Bobbi Brown ever since.

Handing over her business to let someone else scale it up means she has a global brand and was able to create the Pretty Powerful charity to support women and girls.

Being able to sell your company, stay on as the creative head, negotiate a great contract where you have freedom to navigate and grow your brand, and let someone else handle the scaling up – this is one option!

RIP CURL

Wetsuit maker Rip Curl used an ingenious strategy to scale up. Rather than manufacture more wetsuits in Australia and export them around the world as well as sell here, the company patented the technology of the fabric and the manufacturing techniques, and then licensed to a small number of strategically sourced manufacturers around the world. These manufacturers are in countries that have far lower cost structures than Australian manufacturers, and they each distribute to key markets. According to the company's website, currently nine manufacturers globally hold this licence.

Costs of production and distribution are kept down, and Rip Curl focuses on its core value proposition, which is the technology of its wetsuits.

It doesn't need to manufacture. It doesn't need the warehousing and logistics overheads associated with local manufacture. I imagine the managing director spends lots of time on his board in the water, not the boardroom! It's a brilliant brand story and an ingenious business model.

Traps of scaling up

These are three of the most likely traps to avoid when you scale up your business:

1. Your business isn't optimised with systems

As we will explore more in the chapter on Stage 2 (Build Structure), when you scale up you need to be ready with your infrastructure and systems.

I have seen many businesses scale up too quickly without being prepared. They are without good internal systems and they grow their team to many more people in a short period of time. They don't take the time to automate, they don't invest in technology, they duplicate things rather than streamline, and they add people and cost instead of processes. Things quickly become out of control and sometimes chaotic, and the businesses implode and have to scale back for a while.

Lack of systems can potentially ruin your scaling-up efforts, so if you have the opportunity to scale up very fast, you have to address systems.

2. Uncertainty about your business model

You need to be clear about how your model works, how you make money and at what points.

- Is your business structured for business to business (B2B) delivery or business to consumer (B2C)?
- Is it an online model?
- Are you a wholesaler also wanting to be a retailer?
- Are you a manufacturer developing brands for your clients and for yourself?

Systems, technology and people make up your organisation's core capabilities, and these will be geared towards one kind of model.

If you change the model, you change the core capabilities.

It's also essential to understand every step of your process from the time you acquire a client or customer.

Map out the exact things you do for your client or customer at different points in their journey. Are you charging when you do something that adds value to them, or are you missing out on revenue opportunities? This is a worthwhile exercise because you may find your model has some gaps and opportunities.

3. Uncertainty about the levers in your business model

If I were to offer you $2 million to scale up your business fast, would you know what levers you need to invest in for growth? Most business owners tend to think of scaling up in terms of adding more people to their company, acquiring another business or a brand, or adding another office or branch. These are all valid and may work for your business as it is today, but not how a scaled-up version would look like.

A huge lever may be technology that enables you to reach more clients, automate and multiply and reduce the need for more people. Software and apps can enable you to grow the number of users; licensing of methodologies can multiply service delivery capabilities; and processes enable you to duplicate production, creation and delivery.

What are your levers for scaling up? For Bobbi Brown, massive production facilities enabled two levers – an army of development chemists and economies of scale.

Chapter highlights

- It's important to consider your business model – this will influence how you grow through the four stages.
- Scaling up requires resources – people and cash.
- Intellectual property in particular (including technology) enables small businesses to scale up.

CHAPTER 3

Stage 1 – Foundation

THIS stage is critical because your business needs a lot of attention and care so it flourishes and is strong. Building sound foundations is the most important priority.

The Foundation stage may take a few months or several years, depending on the type of business and owner.

More than any other stage, Foundation has a spectrum of levels.

At the lower end is a business without a stable and ongoing client base, where the owner is constantly searching for new business and new clients.

In the highest-level business the owner continues to deliver more value through new products and services to a stable and ongoing client base. New clients are acquired in a considered way because the urgency to bring in more business isn't there.

Advanced Foundation

What I refer to as Advanced Foundation businesses are often more stable and profitable than many businesses struggling with complexity and lack of focus in Stage 2.

Some Foundation businesses become self-supporting through the acquisition, nurturing and continued growth of their client base. In these Advanced Foundation businesses, the business owner may have a few people as a support team and a good income that funds a certain lifestyle. This enables the owner to remain at this stage of growth without the need to step up to the complexity of Stage 2.

Here are some successful Advanced Foundation businesses.

ANNIE – SPECIALIST TRAINER

This solopreneur had come out of a corporate career with considerable specialist expertise and, as people often do, converted that expertise into a service business.

For 10 years, Annie built a successful business that supported her well and delivered tangible, measurable results for her clients.

However, this business created a growing workload for her to acquire new clients by marketing and business development, deliver the services – frequently having to travel by air in order to do so – plus reconcile the work with invoicing and collecting receivables, handling all the associated business admin work and bookkeeping. She was stretched to the limit, worked every weekend and fitted in family and friends in tiny bites.

Annie finally took the plunge and employed a part-time bookkeeper who also handled most of the office admin tasks, and over time she recruited and contracted two suitable trainers to take on certain aspects of the training projects. She started to get more free time, both in her personal life and to have a bigger-picture focus on growing her business.

Most of her clients were on a retainer basis and had recurring projects, which is how she had positioned her services.

At that point she decided to stay in Advanced Foundation and continue the cycle of client acquisition and growth through the funnel of services she had created. She was happy now and decided to stay there with managed and manageable growth. She had reclaimed some of her time and her life with a small team for support and didn't want to move into the complexity of the next stage of growth.

EDWARD – SALES TRAINING

This business was many years in the making. Edward originally built his business through speaking engagements and workshops for industry groups, where he acquired new clients who then referred him to other members.

Most businesses are interested in increasing sales and many need coaching to increase their sales skills, so he was already marketing a service that people not only wanted but needed.

It took several years to build a healthy repeat client base from the primary referral source of the membership group. Edward's clients wanted sales coaching for their team, for individual members and for new salespeople, as well as refresher training. Once his core client base was built, the income from core coaching services funded an enjoyable and comfortable lifestyle. Edward didn't need or desire to grow his business into Stage 2, with its added complexity.

In order to grow his business, he developed some products – account-management tools – which he was able to sell into the same client base. He employed someone else to sell and support these new products and a small group of trainers to teach his coaching programs. When he works with clients one-on-one, he charges a premium for his expertise.

This is a classic example of a successful Stage 1 business – a lifestyle business – that is self-supporting because of the size of the client base, and because there is an ongoing need for the services provided. The owner first built a solid base of clients over several years and provided an ongoing service to the sales teams within those client companies. Then he strategically developed new products and services to supply those clients, always looking for ways to add new levels of value. He has been able to grow his own revenue, and his lifestyle, while helping his clients do exactly the same through increased sales. A perfect Stage 1 business model.

Service businesses and Stage 1

Stage 1 becomes a viable business model for many service providers when they handle it like Annie and Edward did. The downside is that you won't have a large asset to sell, but if you have the right client base you can build your wealth as you go, rather than through the sale of the business.

Factors affecting how long your business remains in Foundation include things like your industry, your specific niche if you have one, your personal drive, your chosen target market and its need for what you're offering and market conditions.

I have had clients who have taken a matter of months to move through Foundation, and others who are still there after 20 years.

Who is in Foundation?

- Business start-ups
- Solopreneurs or businesses with few resources – if any – to support the owner
- Any business that is continually searching for more clients and more revenue in order to survive, regardless of the longevity of the business.

Challenges of Foundation stage

- Build a client base
- Increase cash flow
- Become self-supporting.

Stage 1 businesses universally face these challenges again and again. There will always be a struggle to focus on overcoming these challenges, as it requires hard work and real clarity about the foundations you want to lay for your business.

Build a client base

The main challenge here is to attract and acquire the *right* clients.

What are the right clients?

- Those that need and want what you can offer.
- Those who will pay for your services

- Those who value what you have to offer
- Those you will enjoy working with
- Those you can grow with.

I know from experience that when I have ignored this and worked with clients I personally don't enjoy working with, or who don't really value what I am doing for them, it's a disaster! There is no repeat business, there is no referral, there are issues with fees, and there is no joy.

Increase cash flow

When you're in Foundation, it's hard to be firm about your fees. We have all dropped our fees and prices just to secure a piece of business. But being the cheapest is generally not the path to growth.

Increased cash flow comes from more sales, charging for what you're worth, being creative with how you package and promote your products and being smart with your terms. Better cash flow and increased sales may come from charging more to a smaller client base who can afford your services, rather than acquiring a greater number of clients who can only afford your lowest-priced offering.

Building a business with the right client base is hard to do to start with, because most business owners are too fearful of narrowing their focus and prefer to expand it to include anyone and everyone.

But, when you learn to overcome this natural instinct, you will start to build a more sustainable business.

Become self-supporting

When you have the foundations working you will have achieved a level of sustainability that will enable you to breathe! You can start to think more strategically, plan ahead, and start to shift your thinking from operational business owner to strategic CEO.

Keys to success in Stage 1

- **Clarity about your target market** and not diluting your value by trying to provide the wrong clients with services that are not your true core competency or highest value offer.

- **Having a clear message about who you can help**/work with and the value you add, or solutions you bring to them.

- **Building a client base of repeat customers** as opposed to single-transaction customers.

- **Continuing to innovate for your client base** and provide new services, and products, that will add more value to them and keep them coming back.

- **Being clear about your terms** and structuring them in such a way as to feed, rather than starve, your cash flow.

- **Focusing on your most responsive marketing** channels and activities and continuing to market your business on an ongoing basis, so you always have a pipeline of prospects.

Foundation examples

BECKY – HOMEWARES/CLOTHING BUSINESS

Becky had lots of retail experience and a keen eye when it came to sourcing products to sell. She always wanted to have her own store, and finally found a space to let in a busy shopping strip.

She went into this venture on her own, without any prior experience as the owner of a business. Although she was full of enthusiasm and commitment to her new venture, this alone is not necessarily a recipe for success.

She started out with a homewares store with some furniture pieces as well. The business was successful as it had few competitors in the area at the time. However, within a few years new competitors started to impact Becky's sales and cash flow.

She tried to find new products that would set her apart, and as a result she gradually turned her business into a clothing store – but still had some homewares and pieces of furniture. She put clothes in the window to draw people in, but once inside they were confused as to what the business was all about.

She lost some customers, but acquired new ones who were attracted to the new clothes. Her business always ran close to the wind with cash flow, as all the product had to be purchased from wholesalers before selling to customers. Unfortunately, Becky thought the products were more valuable to the business than the customer base. She failed to actually record any details about her customers. She would easily have had several hundred people on her list, had she done that.

Because she lacked the database she was unable to market special offers, promotions and invitations to her customer base in a strategic way. (This was before social media marketing was really in the mix.) This exercise alone, done well, could have considerably increased her sales and cash flow.

Over time, Becky scrambled to add back homewares products, but in a completely different style to those she had previously stocked. The shop lost its way and eventually closed from lack of focus on the right things, and ultimately lack of cash.

Becky needed to focus on:

- clarity on what her business was (homewares, fashion, lifestyle etc.)
- being known for something in particular (unique positioning)
- regular marketing to her list and to capture new customer names for future promotions
- tight cash-flow management.

ROSS – GRAPHIC DESIGNER

Graphic design – particularly if you specialise in print media – can be a difficult business to be in. It is a highly competitive market full of small studios and solopreneurs, with clients who can take advantage of this situation and haggle you down on price, leaving very small margins. Print media is reducing in the overall marketing mix, leaving those who fail to learn new skills floundering in Stage 1 forever, and those who specialise and build their brand above a commodity service, to thrive and grow.

Ross worked on a freelance basis, subcontracting to different agencies for many years. Gradually he found that the stream of jobs from these sources had dwindled, and he struggled to find work. His main focus was design for traditional print media, which is now a commodity that even untrained people can do using readily available software.

Any business owner who allows their work to be seen as a commodity will struggle and will always be competing on price with the next designer, which is a dark place to find yourself in.

Ross fell into this trap by doing the same thing for 30 years. He wasn't thinking about his clients and how he could potentially grow them and continue to add value to them because he is stuck in the past. He struggled to reinvent his business and innovate with new technology and new services.

Unfortunately, Ross's business was not sustainable and was kept alive by friends providing work when things became dire.

Ross failed to focus on:

- marketing to bring in new clients
- outsourcing to take advantage of people who could have added value with different skill sets
- the market and what other graphic designers were doing and what potential clients wanted
- creating a point of difference and value in a highly competitive market.

JANE – PR FIRM

A lot of people don't really understand PR, so sometimes selling PR services can be difficult as you need to educate the prospective client about PR first, before you get into exactly what *you* can do for them and the outcomes they can expect. Starting with a clear value proposition is the key.

Jane was completely unstructured, unfocused, and unclear on what she wanted to do with her business.

She was heavily reliant on one client, which effectively meant she had created a job for herself as opposed to creating a sustainable business. She was unable to articulate her value proposition, and continued to try and acquire *any* clients that would simply bring in some cash.

She failed to build the foundations that would enable her to grow. She was unclear on the specific services she provided and her value proposition, she was unable to narrow down her focus to define her ideal client, and her business development efforts were ad hoc at best.

Jane would tell anyone who asked how busy she was and how she had so much 'happening' in her business. She was busy because she was disorganised and lacked focus. This may sound harsh but if you're going to grow a business successfully to be a stable Foundation business, or continue growing to the next stage, you must have focus.

Jane was on the hamster wheel and unable to get off. Her greatest failing was not taking the time to get the foundations right so she could build a business. She is stuck in the worst possible part of Stage 1, struggling to get a foothold.

Jane would have benefitted from:

- taking the time to think about what she was doing and what she wanted to be doing
- seeking some input from clients or friends on what they perceived she was really good at
- getting real clarity on what her business was all about – what she offered and for which market
- using really clear messages to communicate with her target market.

MY FIRST BUSINESS – SANTÉ MARKETING

I started my first business – a general marketing consultancy – in response to being stuck in a company whose values and strategies I didn't agree with. There was also a recession and a scarcity of the marketing roles I was looking for.

So I found myself standing in line (yes, before 'the internet') at the Consumer Affairs office, waiting to register my business name. My first choice was taken. My second choice was also unavailable. Not wanting to have to go away and think of an alternative name and go through this whole process again, the name of a restaurant came to mind. It was one I used to go to with my friends on a fairly regular basis, and we loved it. It was called 'Santé'. And so Santé Marketing was born! Nothing strategic for this Foundation business example so far!

I started the business from scratch with no previous clients or contacts to kick start it. I remember how much hard work it was while I was in Stage 1. Like many new business owners, I didn't want to miss *any* opportunities and tried to be all things to all people. I took on a lot of marketing projects that required I outsource work to people like graphic designers and printers, and for a while I was more like a copywriter and project manager coordinating the production of marketing collateral. (Remember, this was the old days.)

I was constantly in business-development mode. When a project finished I had to look for a new client for the next project. It was stressful, hard work and not exactly what I signed up for at the time!

It took a few years but when I finally acquired a large corporate client that enabled me to be a strategic marketing consultant, I was able to charge more. I stopped working with small businesses and focused more on medium-sized companies as clients. My focus shifted to doing what I was really good at – strategy. That was also when I first started mapping out a suite of services I could actually offer my clients that added more value and were a logical flow from one project to the next.

I then had clarity around what my core service offering was and how it added value, what type of client I wanted to work with, and how I was able to charge for my services and generate positive cash flow. It was from that point onwards that I was able to start building my team with part-time staff. I also created a large research-based project (with a strategic partner) targeted at the IT industry. It was a huge success for my business and I could have become known for that and grown an entire business around that on its own.

But as I headed for Stage 2 growth, I had to be completely honest with myself and acknowledge that I was building a business because I *could* (based on my expertise and experience), not because it was actually what I *wanted* to do.

I realised that I hadn't finished my corporate career and headed back into the foray for one last time!

My key lessons from this business were:

- ongoing marketing is everything, and ad hoc marketing isn't enough
- being true to yourself about your unique abilities and your positioning is fundamental to success
- getting a support team – starting with part-time or outsourced support – is essential for growth.

STEPH – PILATES STUDIO

Steph is driven, determined, energetic and positive. As an ex-Olympian, these characteristics underpin her success. She is building the foundations of a successful business and is focused on marketing as the primary driver of growth.

When Steph first started her business she did two things that proved to work well to get her client base up and running. First was to have 'Pilates parties' at friends' houses to build referrals. Friends, relatives and clients would invite their own friends for a private group Pilates session in their home, garden or local park. From those sessions, Steph would get more referrals and opportunities. The other key strategy that helped build her client base was to align with contacts in the sporting and exercise markets to create strategic alliances. For example, she offered to provide a Pilates component to a local golf club running a series of lessons. The course participants would have a golf lesson, then have a half hour Pilates session with Steph. She would always add value after her sessions with a handout covering the mat exercises done, but also a recipe for a healthy snack. She also gave everyone a taste of the different recipes at the end of each session.

If you like this strategy for your own business, remember it only takes one good alliance partner and one client who is a fan to build significantly your connections and clients. Until Steph had a studio, she spent her days driving between conducting classes at clients' homes or outdoors in parks.

Importantly, Steph's initial database was built from personal connections. With so much focus on online marketing and digital media it's easy to forget about the power of personal connections for growing your business.

By the time she eventually found a low-cost studio to get her group classes going, she had developed a sizeable customer database and was able to promote her new classes and offers with regular marketing emails.

Now, she has a new studio – a truly beautiful space where she runs all sorts of classes each day with a number of instructors, and also offers related services such as myotherapy in this space.

Steph created products and programs that her clients wanted, and she focused constantly on the marketing. As a result of this focus, her business has successfully transitioned from Stage 1 to the early stages of Stage 2. Steph's focus was on:

- collecting names and building a database she could market to
- self-promotion and PR from day one
- focusing on referrals from happy clients
- knowing what her clients want and offering new services and products to them.

TOM AND NICKY – TAKE-HOME MEALS BUSINESS

This business does a great job of maximising its retail floor space and converting it to sales revenue. The business essentially provides prepared take-home meals. The shop contains their kitchen where they prepare and cook all the food, and has some seating as well.

They know that most of their customers tend to come in for take-home meals later in the day, so they considered what else they could do to generate sales during the rest of the day.

They started to offer catering, which they use their on-site kitchen for when they have finished the take-home meals. They also provide light food for lunch or snacks during the day, hence the small amount of seating for customers who want to eat in.

But in addition to these services, they also stock their shelves with kitchen-related products from their suppliers, like a small selection of cooking implements, boutique cleaning products for the kitchen (all beautifully packaged), and a selection of candles and room fragrances. Add to that a range of gift cards and you have a go-to store for dinner, lunch, small-scale event catering, and gifts for foodie friends! On top of that, they have started running cooking classes.

Tom and Nicky focused on maximising sales from the space they have. Although they have a lot going on, they are being smart, and as long as they add resources to help deliver all their services, they will keep growing if they want to from Stage 1 into Stage 2.

Tom and Nicky focused on:

- building a customer base for their core offering – quality take-home meals
- leveraging off that customer base to develop more product and service offerings for those customers
- maximising potential sales from the floor space
- knowing what their customers want and giving it to them.

This is a great example of a strategic approach to growth and taking every possible opportunity to expand their customer base and cash flow, and become fully sustainable and self-supporting.

Top 3 strategies to use in Stage 1

- Develop **marketing foundations** to attract potential clients to your business and raise your profile within your target market.
- Manage and increase **cash flow**.
- Use **external resources** to support your growth.

When Foundation businesses have acquired enough clients and built up a reasonably consistent cash flow, and the tree has started to sprout leaves and new growth, the next natural stage of business growth is to Build Structure.

Chapter highlights

- If you don't really want to start and grow a business of your own (although it may be a reaction to something else in your life that is leading you in that direction), then it probably won't be a long-term proposition for you and you will likely stay in Stage 1.
- You *must* have focus on what your market wants and provide that. Be clear about your value proposition and who you are.
- Ongoing marketing to communicate what value you provide and how you are different is essential to survival and growth.
- Bringing other people onboard – even as virtual resources or casual staff – will help you grow without destroying your cash flow.
- Cash is to your business what water is to your body.

CHAPTER 4

Stage 1 Action Plan – Foundation

IN Stage 1, most people aren't thinking strategically about their business, as the main goal is to start generating income. The approach is generally tactical and all about 'now' – today, this week, this month. It's very much a survival mentality. Make one sale or get one client or secure one project or contract, and then look for the next one. Keep the money coming in – these are the overriding thoughts of Stage 1 business owners.

Those with longevity tend to be specialists who have carved out a niche in their market, or are known for offering a product or service that you just can't get anywhere else. Being one of five generalist physios in the same local area will make it challenging to build a practice. Being a *specialist* physio in the same area will make it easier to build your business, as long as your referrals and marketing activities are effective.

To recap, the top three strategies to focus on in Stage 1 are:

- Marketing foundations

- Managing cash flow
- Using external resources to help you grow.

So now let's move onto the action plan for Stage 1 businesses.

Create your marketing foundations

There are five key components of marketing foundations that you must have in place in order to grow your business.

1. Mastery – be clear about how your business delivers real value to your clients and exactly what you do.
2. Market – be clear about who is your ideal client.
3. Message – be clear about communicating your expertise and delivering value.
4. Best-fit marketing – choose the marketing activities and create the marketing content and collateral that are the best fit for you and your business right now.
5. Marketing system – your system will pull all the above elements together to form a consistent program over 12 months. The more you can automate and/or delegate and/or outsource your system the more consistent and therefore effective it will be.

I think many marketing gurus have done small-business owners a disservice by promising that their system is easy and will produce thousands and thousands in sales. These systems are not quick fix strategies, many of them are not at all easy to get right and do well, and they take time to see sizeable results. It doesn't mean they don't work; it's just that in many cases you need a team of experts to help execute the more complex of these strategies.

The reality for most business owners is that they fail to persevere with their marketing because they become disheartened at lack of results, confused about how to do the convoluted multi step

Stage 1 Action Plan – Foundation

sequences taught by marketing gurus, and ultimately become overwhelmed.

The first three components of your marketing foundations are so critical to your success because they give you clarity, focus and intent. In order for your marketing to be effective and for you to get your message across to the right people, you must be clear on what you do, the value you deliver, and who your prospective clients are. Having said that, you do need to have a viable business proposition and there does need to be enough demand in the market for what you deliver, in order for you to build your business.

> The first three components of your marketing foundations are so critical to your success because they give you clarity, focus and intent.

It's fair to forewarn you that getting to the point where you have clarity around your mastery, your market and your core message can take quite a bit of analysis, soul-searching and work. But stick with it because it *will* give you clarity, and that will give you focus. Those things alone will put you ahead of the pack!

My objective with this chapter is to help clarify what you need to focus on with your marketing, and help you to get it right.

First, let's focus on Step 1 of your Marketing Foundations.

1. Mastery = Your value proposition

Your 'mastery' is what you do or deliver that is your unique expertise or product. If you are a solo service provider in Foundation this is a difficult exercise to do because it is very personal – it *is* all about you. If you have a larger service business the process you follow to arrive at your mastery/value proposition is similar, but still equally as challenging.

Defining your mastery or your area of expertise is an essential foundation in marketing. What you deliver and the outcomes you produce largely determine the market you decide to target, and will underpin your messages and how you craft them and communicate them.

While working on this exercise, make sure that there is also a big enough target market for your area of expertise. I once met someone at a business conference who specialised in 'helping people with their energy through using beautiful flowers. I just love flowers!' Not a huge market for that one, I would think.

So back to you. If you're having trouble getting new clients, or you don't think people really understand what your offer is, you may have some fine tuning to do with this foundation piece of your marketing. When you actually communicate what it is that you do, anyone you tell should be able to understand what you mean.

This section on 'mastery' is a large one, precisely because it is so difficult to do and for that reason I've given you two different methods for approaching the exercise. Use whichever one works best for you, or try both.

For example, a consulting firm may advise on sustainability, but its real mastery/value proposition lies in helping government to draft policy and communicate that to key stakeholders in a compelling way. A recruitment firm could define its mastery/value proposition as successfully placing corporate CEOs in the finance industry, for example.

It takes some time and plenty of analysis to really pin down your area of mastery, and everyone has a different way of tackling this challenge. Here is my exercise:

Method 1

A brand design firm may specialise in developing creative ideas, but their real mastery where they add the most value to their

Stage 1 Action Plan – Foundation

clients is in their ability to translate complex technical issues into simple, easy to understand visual concepts. Let's use this method to see how the business owner/brand designer may reach that value proposition.

Step 1 – Make a list of all the things you love to do, and put an asterisk next to those that you're also really good at.

Step 2 – Make a list of all the things you liked to do as a child, and put an asterisk next to those that are in some way related to the activities you listed above. This is relevant only in so far as it provides a reference point back to the theme of 'mastery' that runs through your life.

Step 3 – Make a list of the things you've done for your clients where you've added real value to them and helped solve their challenges and problems. For example, you may create, coach, negotiate, compile, develop, eliminate, simplify, streamline and/ or implement, so they receive tangible benefits and outcomes.

If you don't yet have many clients, refer back to the real value you've added to your employer and colleagues in your career. Be as specific as you can. Make the list as long as you can remember. Highlight or asterisk the areas of value or 'mastery' that keep recurring throughout these three steps. This is the core of this exercise so spend as much time on it as you need and do ask your clients and colleagues for their input.

Step 4 – Imagine you start doing the thing you really love, and you're surprised when you realise how much time has elapsed, as it only seems like just a short while you've been doing it. What is the thing that you could do all day long and enjoy it? Anywhere in Steps 1 to 3 where you've listed 'that thing', circle it.

Step 5 – Combine the items you've asterisked in Steps 1 to 3 with the activity you put down for Step 4. Somewhere in that mix is your mastery.

Identify your mastery – sample worksheet

This example is for the brand design practitioner we referred to earlier.

1. List all the things you love to do, and asterisk those that you're also really good at.	2. List all the things you liked to do as a child, and asterisk those that are in some way related to the activities you listed in Step 1.	3. List the things you've done for your clients where you've added real value to them. If you don't yet have clients, list where you've created most value in your career.	4. What is the thing that you could do all day long and enjoy it?
Draw	Colouring and drawing	Designed and mapped out a new product development system	Convert words and text into images*
Do crosswords*	Play with puzzles*	Converted a business plan into a summary using images only that was sent to all offices globally and was really well received and understood by everyone*	Group ideas into visuals*
Play Sudoku and Trivia	Help my brothers and sisters with their homework – teach them	Designed a prospectus for a high-tech company that attracted investor capital*	Using visual design to communicate concepts and messages
Play tennis	Drawing designs*	Create corporate branding and logos	Designing/ drawing
Organise things into systems*	Play tennis		
Solve problems			

In addition to design and branding, there are common threads shining through:

- systems
- simplifying things
- drawing and converting words to visuals.

When you finesse these threads into what the brand designer could offer, and drill down further to the real value added to clients, an area of mastery emerges.

A clear value proposition could be: 'Simplify complex systems into compelling visuals that clearly communicate meaning and messages.'

This value proposition would appeal to target clients in specific industries. We could sum up this value proposition as: 'Convert complex and technical concepts and ideas into easy-to-understand visuals.'

This design firm now has a clear area of mastery which is its value proposition to a specific target market. That's the other benefit of doing this exercise: it will identify clearly who your target market is.

As I said before, this is a difficult exercise as it requires you to be specific and to narrow down what you *can* do, to what you really *want* to do and what you're *really good at*. It will take several iterations and it will evolve over time. Just give it a go for now to get started.

Method 2

A value proposition is meant to describe the value you provide as well as differentiate you from the competition. The latter is difficult in crowded markets, and it's important to remember that your clients will choose to work with you not just because of your value proposition *statement*, but because of the way your entire business communicates that at different points such as via your website, or via your direct sales approaches or other means.

Here are four steps to help you create your value proposition:

Step 1 – Understand your clients' challenges. List here all the challenges you help your clients with.

Step 2 – List all the value, benefits, outcomes and results you achieve for your clients. If you need help with this, ask some of your clients what they gain from working with you and how you've helped them. If you have a new business and few clients, ask your friends how they see your unique value, or ask some colleagues how you added value when you worked for someone else. When you've finished the list, identify the top few ways that you add the most value to your clients.

The benefits they achieve could be about making money, saving money, reducing risk, saving time, saving them the effort of having to do it themselves, or reducing their worry and stress.

All the results you've provided for your clients up until now will be the core of your value proposition. And if you can state this in their words and not yours it will be far more powerful.

Step 3 – List all of your direct competitors, plus general competitors who offer an alternative to what you do. For example, if you provide an online travel-booking service, you may have specific competitors who do the same thing, or general competitors like travel agencies and hotel and airline online reservation systems.

Now make another list of what makes you different from your competitors in terms of how you deliver value. Once you've done that, highlight the most compelling differences that would add the most value to your target market.

For me, as a strategy advisor to small-business CEOs, my clients could go to many alternative service providers, companies, consultants, franchises, online resource sites and business television programs. The service delivered is different in each case, as is the scope of the service. Of the multitude of alternatives, not one has my experience, my skill sets, my approach, my attitude – and not one of them is actually me! The same applies to you.

We are unique and you need to drill down to why and how you are different from others and what makes 'you'. If you work through this exercise for a large organisation the same applies, and your company can have a personality just as an individual does. Finding that personality is important.

Step 4 – Pull it all together. This is where you need to play around with the words you've pulled out of your lists and try them in different combinations. Start your sentence with 'We help our clients to ...' or 'We provide XYZ that saves/protects/relieves/makes ... for our clients'.

Remember to focus on what your clients really need help with and what you can do for them. It isn't about what you do. What is important is their perspective. You may have a different value proposition for different segments or types of clients. Keep that in mind. For example, if you have a web-design company, you may offer design, hosting, SEO services and email marketing. Depending on what your prospects were looking for, or who you were talking to, you may decide to use the value proposition related to email marketing to help your clients attract more customers, rather than your hosting services.

Jay Abraham gives an example in his marketing book *Getting Everything You Can out of All You've Got*. A consultant was working with a brewery on the value proposition of its beer. At the time there were apparently many brewers in that particular market and it was very difficult to differentiate. The consultant asked the brewer about their process and how they brewed their beers. He was taken through the lengthy and painstaking process of purifying and testing the water they used. The consultant, amazed at this process, was told that it was no big deal because all the breweries used exactly the same process.

But the point was, none of them had ever explained that process to their target market. So this brewery claimed a leadership position in the market, merely by using the story of the 'purity' of their process before anyone else had. That became their value proposition. Beer drinkers must have related to the product completely differently as a result of this new positioning because within six months the brewery's sales had moved it from number eight in the market to number one.

So play around with your words and which combination will be most compelling and meaningful to your target market. Try a few different combinations and test them at networking events or with your clients.

Using the value proposition in your marketing

New prospective clients are more likely to be influenced by what other clients say and how they relate to your value.

Tell your prospects what they want to hear. It's not about you and what you do, it's about what they receive. WIIFM – What's In It For Me – is what every prospective client needs to know above all else. When you have your value proposition well represented in your marketing materials, and supported by client testimonials, the value you provide will be clear.

Remember to support your value proposition with evidence. We all like evidence that the person or the organisation can actually deliver what they claim to deliver. That's why testimonials, case studies and client lists all support the value proposition and reinforce your positioning.

I hope this has been helpful for you – crafting a value proposition is not a straightforward or easy task, but the methods and steps outlined here should help you to identify and craft it.

2. Market = Your ideal client

This is frequently a challenge for most businesses, of any size. In the early stages of your business, your focus is on getting new clients and bringing revenue into your company. Somewhere along the way you decide to only work with people whose values resonate with yours and who you enjoy working with. (I personally think that everyone should take this approach as it makes business enjoyable and rewarding with this kind of alignment.)

A big danger for most businesses is the reluctance to narrow down

Stage 1 Action Plan – Foundation

their target market and to pick one type of client or customer over another. A broad target market means you are trying to be all things to all people, and specialists in nothing. Unless you have unlimited funds, trying to get your marketing out to multiple segments of the market is not cost-effective either. There is no point wasting your marketing efforts on the wrong market.

If you're not crystal clear on your target market, you run the risk of attracting the wrong clients, and doing projects that don't really inspire or engage you. However, if you have been able to identify your mastery and the value you add prior to getting to this step, then identifying your ideal client should be much easier.

> A big danger for most businesses is the reluctance to narrow down their target market and to pick one type of client or customer over another.

The answers to these three questions will help:

1. **Who has the most to gain** from your area of expertise/your mastery? Who has the challenges that your expertise can solve?

   The key here is to link your mastery with your market. There is no point in focusing on the work you love doing if there isn't a market for it. (Remember the 'healing though flowers' example?)

2. **Who will pay the required fees** for your services/products?

   People who are desperately in need of the thing you can provide will pay for it. They will find the funding somewhere. Compare the people who will pay whatever you ask for something they desperately need or want, to those who try and bargain you down. The latter don't truly value what you do, so steer away from them as they are not your ideal target market.

3. **Where are your target clients?** Are you able to reach out to them?

Your target market won't always be neatly grouped into an industry body – like accountants, plumbers, electrical engineers – or into a socio-demographic group like mothers of preschool children. These sorts of groups are easy to find because you know where to go to find them – their industry associations, informal groups on social media, or through specific publications targeted at those groups.

Other target market clients are hard to find because they could be anywhere, like small business owners. This group is massive and needs to be segmented down to sub-groups that can be found and more easily communicated with.

Remember the first two questions

Often there is more than one segment you can target and serve. To start with, if you find yourself trying to work out which segment to focus on first, go back to the first two questions: who has the most to gain from your area of expertise/your mastery because they have the challenges your business can solve? And who will pay the required fees for your service/product?

Being clear about what your business is really good at – and which market you serve best with that expertise – will make your marketing more focused and more effective. It will also be easier to create your core messages. Then when you create your marketing materials, make sure your core message is clear in all your communication.

3. Message = Your content

This alone can become overwhelming if you don't have a strategy to identify, create and use your content. It is often referred to as your 'platform', particularly when your business offering is based on your own area of knowledge or expertise.

Let's go back to our example of the specialist brand design company whose value proposition is to simplify complex ideas and products and convert them into easy-to-understand images. Its core message could be something along the lines of 'design is the core of effective communication.'

The team could break out that core message to a few key principles, and develop content on those principles in a number of ways. They could write articles about their design principles, create visual presentations to represent the same content, covert that to webinars, talks, videos and so on.

I use this method to not only keep me focused on what my core message/core content is, but also to prompt me when I need to create new articles, workshops or speaking outlines that reinforce my core messages.

If you look at my blog – www.jennystilwell.com.au – you will see my core content broken down into key categories: CEO thinking; Growth strategies; Managing growth; Marketing strategies. My overarching primary message is: Better Strategy, Better Business, Better Life. When you have your own business, the ultimate key to enjoying a better life for yourself and those you love, is to make sure you have good strategy.

If you use this method you will be able to create your content more easily. Think of content as 'key topics' and keep drilling down to generate more new content.

Figure 4.1 shows how the design firm could map out its content – main message or topic – with the core message breaking out into sub-messages that can then be broken down further into more specific and targeted content:

Figure 4.1: A design firm's content map (example)

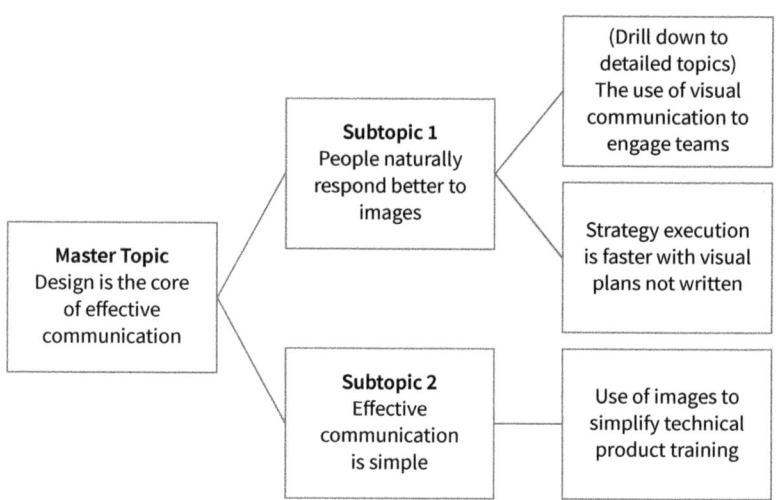

If you take the message of this chapter alone, it could become a core message along the lines of: '5 steps to create your marketing foundations'. Each of the five steps can be broken out into a new message with more information on each step. Your content can keep branching out like in this diagram above.

This content (or topics) – whether it is used in a brochure, on your website, in a presentation or talk, or as the basis of a webinar – is always reinforcing your core message and value proposition.

Consistent adherence to this content, and to consistency in getting out there, will gradually become what you are known for. That is the objective!

4. Best-fit marketing = Confident marketing

This is where so many people go wrong, because they become completely overwhelmed by all the choices and options in the world of online and offline marketing.

Stage 1 Action Plan – Foundation

The key for a business owner in Stage 1 is to use the marketing tools and activities that are the most *natural* for them, and a best fit for their type of business and target market.

Use methods that you are comfortable with. For example, if you like speaking then use public speaking to groups or less public podcasting as a key method of getting your message out to the market. Don't try and write if you find it agonising; don't use social media as a key strategy if you don't know what a hashtag is.

Always ask yourself if the strategies you've chosen are the best fit for you and for reaching your target market.

There are so many different tactics that you can use in your marketing, whether it's using LinkedIn to connect, or posting images of your work and products on platforms like Instagram and Pinterest, writing your own blog, sending out a newsletter, doing webinars and teleseminars, speaking in front of your target audience, networking, creating your own podcast, email marketing, doing product launches, staying top of mind with constant updates on Facebook, trying to be a thought leader on Twitter, using SEO to drive traffic to your site, entering awards to raise your profile in your industry, or hosting events, there is only so much you can focus on.

The key choices you need to make to put together your best-fit marketing program are:

- Decide what options you have in terms of marketing activities
- Decide what corresponding marketing collateral you need
- Select your marketing program menu that you will implement over the next six or 12 months.

When creating your best-fit marketing program, remember to think about your target market and what they read, listen to, pay attention to and notice. It has been a common rule of thumb that most people need to hear/see a marketing message nine times before it actually registers. I think it's probably way more than that now with the constant overload of information we all receive daily. Having said that, consistency in reinforcing your message is essential.

Marketing activities

Keep it simple and achievable and choose between three to five activities from the following list. (This list is by no means definitive but is a good starting point for any business.) Choose your preferred marketing *activities*, both offline and online, as outlined in Table 4.1 below.

My best-fit marketing programs have always entailed writing – no surprise there – so article marketing, blog posts, published articles and learning modules in print publications, digital newsletters and magazines in both digital and print format have underpinned all my marketing. I also enjoy public speaking, but have had most return on investment when I have hosted events specifically for my clients and warm contacts, and have given talks at those events. I have also found that this translates easily for me into video marketing, where I'm again talking to my target market through the video.

The important thing is that because I enjoy these activities and I am comfortable doing them, I have a high level of confidence with these best-fit marketing activities. The goal is for you to find the activities that resonate best with you.

Stage 1 Action Plan – Foundation

Table 4.1: Offline and online marketing activity checklist

Marketing activity	Offline	Online
Advertising – print, outdoor, radio, TV commercials	✓	
Advertising – online (pay per click, Google AdWords etc.)		✓
Article marketing – online sites		✓
Article marketing – print publications	✓	
Direct marketing program – print	✓	
Direct marketing program – digital		✓
Events that you host	✓	
Exhibitions and conferences	✓	
Newsletter – digital or print	✓	✓
Networking	✓	
Podcasting		✓
PR – offline and online	✓	✓
Social media		✓
Speaking engagements	✓	
Sponsorship of events	✓	
Teleclasses		✓
Telemarketing	✓	
Video marketing		✓
Workshops/seminars	✓	
Webinars		✓

Here are some examples of the most common marketing activities for Foundation businesses to attract your target market into your world:

Newsletters to build relationships

- Use monthly calendars printed from Outlook and write in the date for each newsletter for the next six months.
- Make a list in advance of the content you plan to have in each section – feature article, personal update, new product/service information or offer, tips etc.
- If you send one out every week or fortnight you will benefit from a library of articles you've already written that you can draw on when you don't have time to create a new article. To reuse your content, these newsletter articles can also be posted onto your blog to benefit those people who aren't subscribers.
- I have a list of challenges faced by small-business CEOs, and each newsletter I write about one of those challenges. It makes it easy for me to create content rather than be in a mad rush to think of something to write at the last minute.
- Include personal information and photos so your subscribers get to know you. Only do what you're comfortable with so you remain authentic to who you really are. It is important for your prospective clients and customers to get a feel for the sort of person you are, and your personality.

Videos or podcasts

This is simply the audiovisual alternative to building relationships with a newsletter. You do need to have mixed modalities in your communication because we all take in information differently. If possible it is best to combine the written word, videos, podcasts and images to suit everyone's style and attention span.

Stage 1 Action Plan – Foundation

Speeches and talks

- Reuse your content. If you've had a great response to an article, convert that to a talk. An ebook could be turned into a presentation, and vice versa.
- When scheduling in time for this activity, only take the time to talk to your target audience. Don't be hijacked by the wrong target market, just because someone is after a guest speaker and you happen to be available!
- These take time to prepare, organise and follow up. Don't spread yourself too thin. If you want to do 20 a year, remember that you won't have time for many other activities!
- Always do a dry run or two beforehand.
- Remember your marketing foundations – your mastery, your market and your message. Make sure you are using the speaking opportunity to deliver your core message, or a subtopic of your core message, and make sure you will be talking to your target market. There is nothing more energy-draining than delivering your core message to an audience that has no idea what you're talking about – and doesn't care – or having to deliver a talk that is really off-topic for you but what the audience wants to hear. Both scenarios are a complete waste of time for all concerned.

Social media

- In order to gain some traction with social media and raise your profile, you need to provide interesting and useful information, and be active in this space regularly. Posting daily is good, and if you're not a natural at this, delegate it to someone who can do regular updates for you on a daily basis, which will give you a higher profile. If you have to do it yourself then at least schedule it into your marketing diary for three to four times a week.

- The hard part with social media is *what to post,* so I recommend you decide on the type of information you're going to use and then create that content and schedule it in. For example, I have three main categories of information I use: I repost articles from my blog; I post links to new and interesting products or marketing concepts; I provide one-line quotes related to being a small-business CEO. They are the three main categories of information I use, and occasionally I post an image. The articles are written already, I have sources I use to look for interesting new information, and I have enough quotes already written for a month or two of posts. As soon as I structured my social media strategy around three core types of information that I could prepare in advance, it all became simple to execute, rather than a bewildering headache!
- Post other information you find that will be of interest to your target market and followers.
- Remember the principle of repurposing your content? Use content you've already created and break it up into bite-sized pieces for social media updates.
- Again, remember where your target market is. Are they using social media? Which platforms are they using?

Networking

- The most important thing with networking is to know your objectives. Why are you joining a networking group? Do you want to meet like-minded people from your industry or just people in business in general, or do you want to meet prospective clients, or do you want to meet people who could provide their services to help build your business?
- Select two to three groups maximum you think will be good networks to join.

Stage 1 Action Plan – Foundation

- Always try before you buy! Attend some events before you become a member.
- Depending on the rest of your marketing schedule, don't overload on these events as they can take up large chunks of time.
- When you attend an event, always have an objective on the day. Is it to meet a specific person, or to connect with a certain number of prospective clients, or to get to know one or two people a little better? If you can meet and get to know the founder(s) of the network, that's a great connection to make and a good networking event objective to have.
- Most people with Foundation businesses attend networking events to meet prospective clients. Everyone is trying to do the same thing so make sure you stand out and have your marketing foundations in place and clearly convey the value you can add to your clients. Dress really well.
- Personally, what has always worked best for me in terms of generating new business opportunities is one-to-one meetings and networking. These connections are your own contacts from your own network, people you may have been referred to by others, and people you have been introduced to by mutual connections. Rather than 'connecting' on social media, connect in the real world over a coffee and a chat.

Article marketing

Article marketing is a great marketing strategy if you like to write. You can write one article and use it as content in several ways:

- in your newsletter
- on your blog
- alter the content, title and headings so it's different from the original, but the message is the same, and submit to a print publication

- convert to an ebook – depends on size and topic
- break up the key points and use as mini 'bites' to post on social media
- use it as the foundation of a presentation or talk.

Others' blogs

If you pick the right sites with enough traffic, it's a great way to send traffic back to your site, but again, the article needs to be an original or, at least for Google, not the same as another article you've written.

Print and online publications

Submit articles to the editors. Check their readership distribution to make sure you are optimising your potential reach.

Here are my top three recommendations for the best general article directories and article marketing sites:

- www.evancarmichael.com
- www.business2community.com
- www.ezinearticles.com

Here are examples of my own pages in the top three sites listed above:

- www.evancarmichael.com/Marketing/5309/summary.php
- www.business2community.com/author/jenny-stilwell
- www.ezinearticles.com/?expert=Jenny_Stilwell

Marketing collateral

In terms of marketing collateral, you have the more traditional options of physical pieces like brochures, newsletters, catalogues, print ads and direct marketing pieces. But content marketing is vital, which involves creating some 'content' of value and then using the appropriate online and offline channels to deliver that

Stage 1 Action Plan – Foundation

to your target market. There is an overlap in traditional marketing collateral and content which will be a key part of your marketing activities.

Both of the lists in Table 4.2 below are by no means exhaustive, but they offer a cross-section of online and offline ways to send out your message.

Table 4.2: Offline and online marketing collateral and content checklist

Marketing activity	Offline/ print	Online/ digital
Articles	✓	✓
Audio – MP3 files; podcasts		✓
Blog (and social media) updates		✓
Book	✓	✓
Brochure	✓	✓
Copies of PR/awards/magazine layouts and advertising	✓	✓
Catalogues/product listings/look books	✓	✓
Direct marketing letters	✓	
Ebook		✓
Email marketing templates		✓
Information kits (for prospects and enquiries)	✓	✓
Newsletter	✓	✓
Photo [gallery]	✓	✓
PowerPoint presentations	✓	✓
PR kit	✓	✓

Marketing activity (Cont'd)	Offline/ print	Online/ digital
Product displays	✓	
Product/service overviews/descriptions	✓	✓
Promotional giveaways – e.g. mugs, caps, umbrellas, gift bags (link with events)	✓	
Research report (and publish your findings)	✓	✓
Signage – external; floor-stand 'banners'	✓	
Signature talks	✓	✓
Social media updates/posts		✓
Testimonials from clients and business partners	✓	✓
Tweets		✓
Videos		✓
Website		✓

Each of these will apply to different kinds of businesses. All businesses will require a mix of online – digital – and offline – print or tangible – collateral. Every business must have some online presence whether it be a blog, website or social media platform.

Most Stage 1 businesses will need to be mindful of cost to produce marketing collateral, so choose wisely and really give thought to what will have the most impact with your target market and how you want to position your business.

Only select the key things you need from this list and align them with your marketing activities. If you plan on doing public speaking, then you need a signature talk. If you plan on doing article marketing, then you will need a handful of articles to get started.

Remember, keep it simple.

Marketing program menu

Start with the Marketing activity column. You've already decided on your marketing activities, so just highlight them here. The purpose of this table is to write in the specifics of what you plan to do. For example, if you are going to do print advertising to promote your business, write down the publications you will advertise in. Also make a note of the frequency and the cost.

If you plan to do article marketing, you may select some of the online sites I listed in the Marketing activities section and you may submit an article a week. Write down all the specifics of your marketing activities in Table 4.3 overleaf. The purpose of doing this is that it will feed into your marketing system in the final step of creating your marketing foundations.

5. A marketing system = Bringing it all together

Now we are at the final component of your marketing foundations: the marketing system. This section will cover how to put together the previous four steps into a system that results in regular and continuous marketing for your business.

Your marketing foundations will become a marketing system if you plan what best-fit activities you're going to engage in consistently and frequently, if you have the content already created, and if you have a schedule of when these activities are to take place.

The final step in making this a system is to automate it and/or have someone do it for you. So, for example, you may decide to use a mix of activities including:

- a regular article on your blog post
- repost that article onto your social media platforms
- repost that same article onto social sites of which you are a member, e.g. business groups, or network groups on LinkedIn.

Table 4.3: Marketing activity template

Marketing activity	Detail/ specifics	Frequency	Cost estimate
Advertising – print, outdoor, radio, TV commercials			
Advertising – online (pay per Click, Google AdWords, etc.)			
Article marketing – online sites			
Article marketing – print publications			
Direct marketing program – print			
Direct marketing program – digital			
Events that you host			
Exhibitions and conferences			
Newsletter – digital or print			
Networking			
Podcasting			
PR			
Social media			
Speaking engagements			
Sponsorship of events			
Teleclasses			
Telemarketing			
Video marketing			
Workshops/seminars			
Webinars			

Stage 1 Action Plan – Foundation

- convert the article content into a regular podcast – weekly, fortnightly, monthly
- do a press release once a month to relevant press release sites online and to offline media contacts
- attend a business group networking event once a month
- submit articles to editors of print and online publications every two to three months
- aim to have regular monthly speaking engagements.

With these activities it is easy to schedule them into a calendar over 12 months, or break it down into every three months.

If you have the articles and the press releases ready to go, three months at a time, the only thing you can't automate or delegate is to attend the networking functions and the speaking engagements. I highly recommend that you use a virtual assistant to do this for you. Resources are covered at the end of this chapter.

So, a marketing system is the best-fit marketing activities, the schedule, having the content ready, and getting someone else to do it for you and get it into the world of your target market. If you measure your marketing results, and you should, you will know what activities bring clients into your business most effectively, and you can fine tune and repeat that activity again and again. Google Analytics will show you the sources of your website traffic, including 'referred' traffic from other sites where you have had content published and visitors have clicked on that content to end up on your site.

You can assess the effectiveness of speaking events by the interest you receive and the results you are able to achieve on follow-up. You will be able to measure the results from most of your marketing activities over time.

The best consistent marketing systems can be relied on to deliver results, which are of huge benefit to your business now, and to anyone looking to buy it in the future. Good marketing systems add a lot of value to any size of business. They take some effort to set up and develop content, and some time to bring leads in on a consistent basis, but be patient and persevere – you will see results.

The key to bringing it all together is to keep it as simple as you can, develop plenty of content, and delegate wherever possible.

- Plan ahead – An easy way is to use Microsoft Outlook and print out one month to a page. For example, if you do a newsletter, write in the dates you will send it out and either delegate, or if you're really great at doing this activity and can do it quickly, then do it yourself and schedule newsletters to go out on particular future dates automatically.
- Repurpose your content – If you write an article, you can post it to your own blog; you can send it out in your newsletter; post the link on your social media platforms; convert it into a talk; change it slightly and turn it into an ebook; turn it into a presentation and post onto SlideShare and/or deliver in-person to an audience, turn it into a podcast; use it as the basis of a video, and so on. Do it once, reuse it many times to maximise your reach with one piece of content.
- Identify where you need support resources – You may need help setting up and sending out a newsletter, or help to record, edit and post videos to YouTube or your website. If you've chosen the right marketing activities that are going to promote you and your business, then investing in some virtual or part-time resources to help you is a sound investment.

It's really difficult to coordinate everything and make it all piece together. It's also easy to be overwhelmed by the complexity of it all. Once you have worked through each of these steps to create

Stage 1 Action Plan – Foundation

your marketing foundations, all you need is someone to make it happen each week and each month.

Simply transfer the items from your marketing program and into a calendar (Table 4.4 overleaf). You can even colour-code them so you can see at a glance what you have to do and what your assistant(s) will do.

I can't say it enough: the key to success in Stage 1 is to spend the necessary time working through these five steps to create your marketing foundations, start with a few activities, schedule them into a calendar, and get help to make sure things get done. Most importantly:

So, a marketing system is the best-fit marketing activities, the schedule, having the content ready, and getting someone else to do it for you and get it into the world of your target market.

- Don't overwhelm yourself with too many different marketing activities.
- Keep your messages and your content consistent and always reinforcing your value proposition to your target market.
- If you miss a date in your calendar, it's not the end of the world. This will definitely happen! Just keep going next week.

You can refer back to this system at any time in the growth of your business. Revisiting your marketing foundations may be the starting point when you're planning for business expansion; if your growth stalls at any point you can go back to your marketing foundations and take stock of where you need to focus again to reignite growth. It's a system, so you can use it again and again as required to keep your growth on track.

Table 4.4 Annual marketing activity calendar

Marketing activity	Jan	Feb	Mar	Apr	May	Jun	Jul	Aug	Sep	Oct	Nov	Dec
Advertising – print, outdoor, radio, TV commercials												
Advertising – online (pay per Click, Google AdWords, etc.)												
Article marketing – online sites												
Article marketing – print publications												
Direct marketing program – print												
Direct marketing program – digital												
Events that you host												
Exhibitions and conferences												
Newsletter – digital or print												
Networking												
Podcasting												
PR												
Social media												
Speaking engagements												
Sponsorship of events												
Teleclasses												
Telemarketing												
Video marketing												
Workshops/seminars												
Webinars												

Stage 1 Action Plan – Foundation

Manage your cash flow

Sales revenue

I was talking to a copywriter at an event once, and she excitedly told me that she had increased her number of clients in the last 12 months by 13. That took her total number of clients to 44. I don't know if they were all active, but she shared that most clients spent about $1500 on average each year. There aren't enough hours in the day to service 44 one-on-one clients properly, but even if there were, she would only be making around $66,000 a year.

I asked her if she took her clients on a journey and proactively offered to help them with other related services. This would narrow down her business to those clients who really wanted to continue working with her and for whom she would probably become a key resource, and also those who would add the most value to her business. She would be able to significantly reduce her workload and number of clients, while making more.

She clearly wasn't happy about the prospect of letting any clients go, and didn't see how she would have the time to add any new services as copywriting kept her so busy.

This is just a classic mindset for many Foundation businesses. Not letting go keeps them tethered to the wrong clients and less income, with little joy.

Let's do some quick calculations:

CASE STUDY 1 – MARGARET, ORGANISATIONAL CHANGE CONSULTANT

Margaret was struggling finding new clients, so she offered her services as a trainer to a national training body. The company paid her $800 per session and charged its client between $1500 and $2000 for the day.

Margaret was an extremely qualified and experienced organisational change consultant, but she struggled with structuring her services to be paid what she was worth. She had an opportunity to do some consulting work that was a perfect fit for her skills with a large organisation that matched her profile of an ideal client. Her initial approach was to go in with a daily fee of $1200 for about eight days ($9600).

We mapped out from beginning to end – leaving no part of the process unturned – exactly what she would be doing for this company to help it with its challenges. We broke her service offering down into four components:

- the initial review phase
- the scoping phase for what she recommended for the group of people concerned
- the delivery of change workshops; and
- the follow-up presentation to different groups in the organisation.

We named each component of her proprietary process and priced each stage accordingly. For that process and approach, she put in a proposal with a fee of $28,000.

She won the job. She was so excited – she had never charged this much for a project, although as an employee in other companies she had been charged out at this sort of rate or more.

Compare $9600 for eight days with $28,000. She received close to $20,000 more AND her perceived positioning and value to the client was considerably more than the original 'daily rate' offer that anyone could have provided.

CASE STUDY 2 – MAX AND NADINE, GRAPHIC DESIGNERS

A graphic design firm was struggling with both cash flow and workload. Restrictions on revenue meant the partners were unable to employ anyone, even on a part-time basis, to help. We went through a similar process to Margaret's, and mapped out Max and Nadine's process with clients.

It became evident that they weren't charging for a big chunk of work because they didn't know how to cover those costs without raising their hourly rate considerably. They were attached to the hourly rate of billing, so we had to work around that.

I had them charge a project management fee on all their projects. This was something that could be itemised and easily justified to clients – they could see where that fee went in terms of services being provided.

Stage 1 Action Plan – Foundation

The next thing we did was increase their hourly rate by just 10% to start with. They weren't comfortable with anything more, but they did follow through and charge the new fee on all projects. We also improved their cash flow by changing their billing process to continue throughout the project, rather than invoicing in full at the end.

Those two actions increased their sales revenue by almost $50,000 over the next year. It was more than enough to employ some part-time help.

Cost of goods sold (COGS) and margin

If you are a service firm your cost of goods is how much it costs for the person or people to do a project or provide a service. Accordingly, the time you take will determine how many you are able to do over the course of a year.

If you take 10 clients and deliver the service all at once in a workshop or at a strategic retreat, you are being more efficient in how you deliver and theoretically – if you wanted to – you could repeat this process and serve many more clients in groups than you could one-on-one. This is the most efficient delivery model. Having said that, clients will pay a premium if you create and deliver a workshop specifically for them.

The more efficient you are in your processes the more money you will make. Fewer errors will occur, less rework will be required, projects will be completed ahead of time or on time and you can invoice sooner. Cash flow is tied to efficiency. If you have a product-based business, make sure your margins enable you to make money.

The table below illustrates an example of how different supplier pricing can impact a retailer's margins. Have a look at all your suppliers and whether they have a published RRP or whether they let you use your discretion at pricing their products for your business. Once you've added freight and delivery charges and amortised those across the number of units in the delivery, your margin is already reduced.

Table 4.5: Example of three different supplier pricing options

	Supplier A ($)	Supplier B ($)	Supplier C ($)
Wholesale price	19.50	19.50	17.50
Freight – amortised across quantity of units	0.55	0.55	0.55
Total cost to your business	20.05	20.05	18.05
RRP (where supplier stipulates price you must charge)	39.95	N/A	N/A
Your RRP	N/A	49.95	49.95
Your margin	**19.90**	**29.90**	**31.90**
Replacement cost	20.05	20.05	18.05
'Round 2' margin	**(0.15)**	**9.85**	**13.85**

When you've sold some products and need to replenish them you reorder. If your margin from the first order is less than the replacement cost per unit, you have already lost money – refer to Supplier A.

Supplier B will result in better margins for your business and wherever possible you should choose to work with suppliers who offer you lower cost of goods and/or the opportunity to price the product at a retail price that makes you money – see Supplier B.

Supplier C offers the best outcome for your business. The cost of the product is lower than the other two suppliers, there is no published recommended retail price so you can price the product how you want, so the margin is much better. This is the outcome that all product-based businesses look for, which is why people choose to source lower cost product from other countries, or make their own.

Stage 1 Action Plan – Foundation

Another option when trading in products may not affect your cost of goods but it will be better for your cash flow. If a supplier is able to offer you products on consignment, you don't need to pay for them in advance and you can pay for each one as the customers pay you.

There are all sorts of products that suppliers may be willing to provide you on consignment, so it's always worth asking.

Charge what you're worth

As we've seen from our examples, setting fees is always a difficult proposition for service businesses and professional service providers. Pricing an intangible is much harder than pricing a product.

Setting fees that will represent what you are worth, and make money for your business, is based on good judgement, knowing your client, having a good sense of self-worth and also knowing what your options are.

Service fee options

Hourly fee

This option pays you for your time. This is not advisable as it is severely limiting to the growth of your business, and affects your perceived value with your clients.

As a consultant, I have 30 years of experience that solves problems, takes my clients on a growth path and helps them achieve success. I don't always turn my thinking on and off and many times have solved a problem with insight that comes to me in a moment. Do I charge for the 'moment'?

On the flip side, I see some consultants and professional service providers in particular, recording every six minute block of time and billing their clients part of an hourly fee for that. Each professional in the firm, and every support person, only has so many hours in a day, week, month and year. They reach their limit of billable hours and then need to add a new resource to the firm. As a client, I always wonder if I'm being billed as I chat on the phone to my accountant and he asks me about my holiday – tick, tick, tick…

I have had clients who could honestly remove 60% to 80% of their client base and focus on growing the remaining clients, doing so with less people, less overheads, less stress and more profitability. But they don't because they're caught in the cycle of billing dollars for time.

If you *are* tied to this form of billing, don't forget to raise your fees from time to time. I have had clients who have not raised their fees for five years, simply because they didn't know how, or didn't think they could justify it.

If you don't raise your fees, you are sending a message out to your clients that you're not worth it, are of lesser value than others, or are just not up to it.

Contingency/success fee

This often comes to play when your service is helping a client to win a major piece of business, tender or project. If you charge a fee contingent upon success, you will only get paid when the client wins the business, although you are certainly backing yourself! Don't forget the time lag between you delivering the service and your client winning the project, starting the project, and delivering their first invoice for the project! Also, there are many things that can affect the outcome over which you have no control. It is far better to charge for the service, and if the stakes are high, charge a success fee on top of that. It's like a bonus for exceptional performance.

Stage 1 Action Plan – Foundation

Project fee

When you are involved in a project, whether it's helping a client win a tender, developing a suite of marketing collateral, undertaking a customer survey, or installing new accounting software into their business, you can charge a project fee.

The best way to do this is in staggered tranches. For example, you will always be paid faster if you don't start the project until you receive the commencement fee. If the project is to take five months, for example, and you leave the bulk of the amount to be invoiced at completion, you may not be paid for eight months.

A better progress payment option is 50% upfront, 30% at completion of a (pre-agreed) major milestone, and the remainder on completion of the project. Alternatively, you may decide to invoice 50% upfront and 50% on completion if it is a relatively short project. Never leave the bulk of the fees to be invoiced at the end of the project.

Retainer

A retainer is the ultimate goal of all people in the service profession. There are many forms for different types of services: monthly fee retainer for the provision of ongoing consulting/advisory services, monthly support fee (for software), monthly licence fee, monthly fee to be available on request for support/training, and so on.

You may decide to charge a retainer on a monthly or quarterly basis in advance. Do not enter into a retainer arrangement where you are paid after the service has been delivered. You could end up delivering three months of service and wondering when you will be paid.

If your clients really need your help, they will accept your terms – terms that are agreeable to you!

What are you worth?

This is the Achilles heel of all service providers, because it's all about your knowledge, your capacity to think and be creative or solve problems, and it's based on your accumulated knowledge of usually many years. It also is based on your own sense of worth.

When you deliver value to your clients, help them achieve their goals and solve their problems, you can justify your fees based on that value they receive.

If you are creating a new brand design and marketing collateral for a client, which in the longer term will achieve results like higher market profile, higher-value clients and higher-value business, then what you are delivering has enormous value beyond the time you spend creating it.

I ran a CEO group Mastermind Program many years ago. We set the first membership fee at $300 per month. It barely covered costs. About two years later, with my heart in my mouth I increased the fees to $600 per month. A year later we recruited new members for $1200 per month – no resistance. The members in the program valued it highly.

Keep raising your fees until you feel some resistance, then you know you're close to an optimum level at that time. We increased our program fees 300% based on that strategy.

When I started my first consultancy firm, I did a competitive analysis of other small and midsized consulting firms in the market and the fees they were charging. I set my fees at the lower end of that scale because I was just starting (not because I knew less or would add less value). That strategy is not a recipe for success or growth, unless you are marketing a commodity service to a mass market. It wasn't long before I changed from hourly fees to charging for value and outcomes delivered.

Packaging value

A great way to move toward a value-based pricing model is to bundle products and services together.

If you are an accountant, you could charge a monthly fee, for example, for compliance and BAS services, annual company return, and four quarterly review meetings per annum with the client. You could also package special reporting packs, the individual's personal tax return, their family's annual tax returns, management of their superannuation and a range of other options that suit different types of clients. You could have three basic levels of package starting from $500, up to $1500 per month, as an example. Other clients may opt to remain on an hourly fee, if you decide to give them that option.

That helps with forecasting your revenue, your resource requirements and your profit estimates. Clients know where they stand and exactly what they will receive, and you don't need to have everyone in the firm record their activities at six-minute intervals.

Credentials raise value

When you have a track record of getting results for your clients, your advice is highly valued by those clients and they are happy to tell others, and you have a credible client base that mirrors the sort of clients you are trying to win over and attract, then you are in a position to raise your fees and charge what you're worth.

As guru marketer Jay Abraham says, reduce or remove any obstacles that potential clients may have in dealing with you. Once they become clients, as you deliver value and build your relationship, you can then increase the value of those clients to your business (and increase your fees) over time.

Provide standard and premium offers

If you provide three options, most people will fall into the second one. They don't necessarily want to pay the highest price for the most features and benefits, but they also don't want the cheapest option.

Having two or three versions in your offer at different price points will increase your revenue without you having to feel pushy and self-promoting. Your customers will self-select and with a standard and a premium option, even if only a small percentage of prospects take up the premium offer, you have already made more.

At one point in my consulting business we had two active membership programs: Accelerate and Mastermind. The cost of running Mastermind was marginally more than Accelerate, but the fees were considerably higher. We actually had more Mastermind members over the years than for our other less expensive program.

Positioning dictates fees

If you really do have the capabilities, track record, skill set and experience that make you stand out from the crowd, you can use that to position yourself at the top end of the market. You will aim for bigger and better clients who have the ability to pay the fees you demand and the expectation that quality services come with a high fee.

If you are aiming for that market, but you don't yet have the credentials, remember Jay Abraham's strategy for removing obstacles and go in lower with a view to raising your fees in time.

Don't be too cheap – it raises alarm bells. Don't be too expensive too soon – it will price you out of the market.

Getting your positioning right takes time, as you become more

Stage 1 Action Plan – Foundation

aware of your specific target market and the sorts of clients you want to attract, and how far you can raise your fees in exchange for the outcomes you deliver. Take time, monitor it, and be clear about where you want to be positioned.

Don't be too cheap – it raises alarm bells. Don't be too expensive too soon – it will price you out of the market.

Your biggest hurdle

Don't forget the power of your mindset in charging fees that create value in *your* business! The biggest hurdle that most service professionals face is their own perception of the value of their knowledge.

If you can't get through this you will need a friend, an ex-colleague, a mentor, a business partner, or anyone who has experienced the value you can add to others to reinforce this with you. Someone else's opinion will have more of an impact on you than your own.

A really good strategy is to make a list of the contributions you've made to your clients' businesses, and if you don't have a lot of clients yet then go back through your business career and list the value you've added, the results you've produced, the rewards and recognition you've received for a job well done. Use this list to remind yourself as often as you need. This works whenever you need a confidence boost too!

When you produce results and generate outcomes for others, you should be positioned at the higher end of the scale.

Charge for what you're worth

If prospective new clients try to force you into a 'money for time' situation, don't go there. You have value to offer the right clients who will pay you for what you're worth.

Part of your business growth strategy should also be to seek out clients who not only value what you can do for them, but can also afford it. If you find a potential new client who wants your help, but can't agree to your terms or your fees, you should either reduce the service and so reduce the fee accordingly (i.e. reduce the 'package' you are offering), or walk away.

Forget charging for your time, and start charging for all the knowledge, experience, ideas, capabilities, contacts and resources you have that will ultimately deliver exactly what your clients want, and reward you in the process!

Terms and cash flow

When business owners experience cash-flow difficulties, there is usually one of two responses: immediate rallying (some may use the word 'panic') to address the situation, or denial. Neither are particularly effective strategies.

I have seen denial in action and it solves nothing – it actually makes the situation far worse, pulls your business back and in some cases puts the whole viability of the business at risk – and does nothing to raise the bar on your skills as a business owner. Panic is just as bad as it has you clutching at anything in the hope of improving the situation.

Cash-flow difficulties only go away if you address them, and if your difficulties aren't too dire, there are some simple, proven steps to improve your position.

1. Assess your current position – do a cash-flow forecast

You have to know your exact financial position, so you can manage it. The cash-flow forecast is a spreadsheet by month – the most usual timeframe for service-based, non-retail businesses – that shows when cash will need to go out of the business (payments to creditors) and when you expect it to come in (payments to you). The bottom line is a net surplus or deficit. If you don't know how to do a cash-flow forecast, download one or ask your bookkeeper or accountant to send you a template.

Stage 1 Action Plan – Foundation

Make sure you know what all your expenses are over the next few weeks and remember to include them. Know what income you can expect over the same period of time – not when you invoiced your clients, but when you expect them to pay you. For example, you may have invoiced a client two months ago, but know that they will pay you by the end of the month.

2. Track hidden costs

Automatic debits from your account or business credit card are easily forgotten. These could include insurance, memberships, subscriptions, interest payments and lease payments for car, computers, etc. Some may be more cost-effective to pay for 12 months in advance, rather than monthly, when your cash position is good.

Don't forget costs like ATO payments – BAS, instalments, etc. – as well as superannuation payments. Many of these can be moved around to a time that suits you.

3. Make arrangements with everyone

You can pay any bill later than the due date by making an arrangement with the service provider – you can do this for the phone bill, the tax office and most others. Institutional service providers are more lenient as they have thousands of customers; smaller service providers, like your bookkeeper or graphic designer, will be less flexible. By making arrangements to pay at new due dates, you are able to move around your payments to coincide with money coming into your account.

Don't forget about credit rating – you don't want to extend beyond their timeframes and into what is categorised as being in default, which can potentially impact your credit rating – so make sure you stick to agreed payment plans.

Always communicate on an ongoing basis, especially if you need more time, but *never* stop communicating with your creditors when you have cash-flow problems – that is the worst thing to do.

4. Increase fees by 10%

This may not help immediately with existing clients and projects, but can be implemented immediately for all new clients. If you haven't increased your fees for a while, you should do this anyway as good business practice. Small increases can help improve your cash flow quickly, particularly if you still insist on charging by the hour. If you work with me at any point, hourly fees will become a thing of the past!

5. Arrange retainers

If you do work on a regular basis for any of your clients – and ideally you do – you can propose that you shift your arrangement to a retainer. This will give you monthly income rather than waiting for potentially months to be paid after you've provided the service. I highly recommend this strategy as a standard business practice for service businesses wherever possible.

6. Charge upfront fees

This is a fairly common practice, so if you haven't done it before, you do need to start. It is a good strategy if you charge retainers or if you charge a project fee, which is typically a percentage to commence a project and a percentage on completion. The longer the project, the better for you if you charge more upfront, with one or two progress payments, so the bulk of the fees come to you quickly. It works even better if you combine it with the next strategy.

7. Exchange discounts for earlier payment in full

If a client elects to pay in full, for example, you will give them a discount. This is an effective strategy to improve your cash flow quickly, but don't be tempted to give it all away.

The size of the discount is directly related to:

- how responsive the client is to reducing their costs
- how large your overall fee is
- how urgently you need the cash.

A 10% to 20% discount is reasonable – it's enough of an incentive to most clients, plus it is a cost to you but consider it a cost of acquiring cash. If you are going to offer this, do some calculations first with different discounts to determine what you would be happy with.

8. Set terms and follow up

Whatever terms you decide on, make sure they're adhered to. Always follow up to make sure you're paid – some companies will pay their creditors in order of who is most demanding. If you don't want to follow up, have someone do it on your behalf. I highly recommend to solo professionals that you find someone to follow up on your behalf, so you can look after the client. Have someone else interface with their accounts department.

9. Grow clients

When you need more business, the golden rule is always to revisit your existing/previous clients.

- Do they need a refresher?
- Do you have a new service to offer them
- What ways can you add more value to their organisation?

Do you have any inactive clients who you need to reactivate? Spend some time to think about your client base, and what you can do for them.

10. Find your friends

Get out there and talk to everyone. Where appropriate, ask for referrals or introductions to increase your potential leads; meet with 'connectors' to increase your contact base.

11. Spend time on marketing

This is the best strategy for bringing in new income from new business. The best time to start is when you have plenty of clients and you don't have a cash-flow problem. Build your pipeline of prospective new business today as insurance for tomorrow.

Finally, stay calm, stay focused on what you have to do to sort out your cash flow, then focus on getting new business and increasing your revenue in the next 90 days.

Use external resources to support your growth

Foundation businesses will never grow if the owner of the business tries to do everything themselves. Even if you are happy growing to an Advanced Foundation level and staying there, you won't have much time to enjoy your life if you are doing everything on your own.

So, either way, at some point, you have to bring in some help.

Identify where help is required

In order to get help, you need to know where you need it most. Foundation businesses mainly employ their first support resources in these areas:

- bookkeeping
- marketing assistant
- admin assistant
- sales lead generation support.

You may need help in a different area, but for most Foundation businesses, particularly service businesses, help is usually required in areas that are not the business owner's core competency.

Marketing is a primary focus when you're in Foundation, so it's not surprising that help is required for some of your marketing activities. Once you've decided on your core marketing activities from the menu in the previous section, you can decide which of those activities you need help with.

Do a resource map

A useful tool is what I call a resource map. Working through this really simple process will help you to identify your resource *gaps*.

You can keep it really simple and do a pie chart of all the different functions relevant to your business, then list all the activities that need to be done under each of those functions as shown in Figure 4.2 below.

Figure 4.2: Business resource map

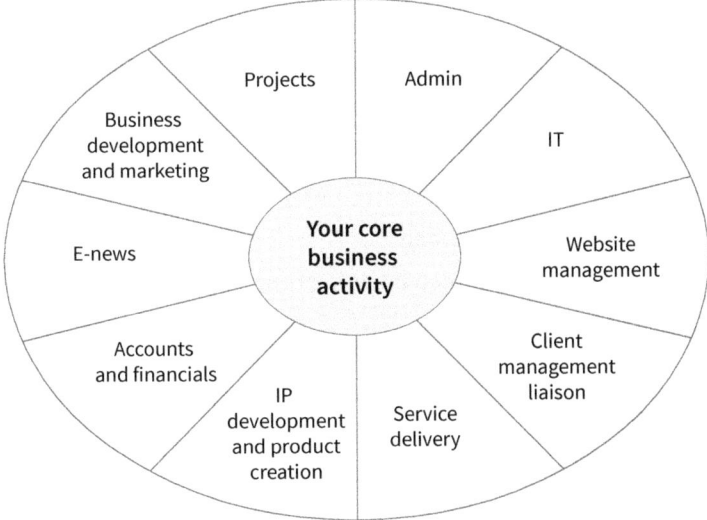

Here's a sample of when one of my companies was in Foundation. We broke all the core activities down, as some of them required different types of resources and skill sets. For example, administration included office management and personal assistant activities to support me in organising my personal priorities, as well as admin support to help manage our mentoring programs.

Business task list – sample

Admin – office management

- Stock stationery and supplies
- Liaise with service providers – Telstra, IT, bookkeeper, accountant, etc.
- Maintain office interiors and presentation
- Organise events – logistics, liaise with venues and others; manage RSVPs.

Admin – PA

- Manage diary
- Arrange travel
- Make personal arrangements – car services, home maintenance, personal appointments, etc.
- File and organise office
- Client communication
- Check and reply to email
- Manage personal paperwork/accounts when required.

Admin – program management

- Liaise with participants in our programs
- Prepare kits and content
- Liaise with any external providers as required.

Marketing/admin backup

- Mail merge for event invitations or direct mailouts
- Convert documents to PDF as required
- Transcribe interviews and other audio as required

Stage 1 Action Plan – Foundation

- Update social media profile/content as required – Facebook, LinkedIn, Twitter
- Upload new updated content to website
- Produce quarterly magazine
- Produce enews and distribute fortnightly
- Produce email campaigns and distribute for promotions
- Submit articles to various sites and publications
- List in business directories.

IT

- Troubleshoot
- Source and install hardware and software
- Technical support
- Set up backup on each PC and network.

Website management

- Modify/upgrade site
- Troubleshoot
- Host web and email.

Client management/liaison

- Set and confirm appointments
- Select gifts when appropriate
- Send out information/documents/preparation materials as required
- Manage invitation lists and event replies when appropriate
- Send welcome gift and note to new clients
- Send thankyou gift and note to referring clients/contacts
- Add to client database of details – kids' names, dogs, partners, hobbies, etc.

- Send updates on new offers/programs, etc. to be followed up
- Organise card-sending service for new clients; new program members; thankyous for referrals.

Service delivery (our programs)

- Individual mentoring
- Team mentoring
- Consulting
- Workshops.

IP development and product creation

- Develop primary content
- Develop product outline brief for content drafting
- Collate program content into end-user format
- Design product cover and packaging for online
- Record audio for CDs to go with product
- Edit audio
- Burn to CD
- Collate printing and binder with content/CDs fulfilment
- Create/design sales pages with professional copywriter
- Register domain names and trademarks if necessary
- Post sales page, product package picture to website
- Update shopping cart with info
- Manage print/production of product units
- Set up autoresponder to provide receipt and thankyou page.

Accounts and financials

- Enter data into MYOB
- Provide month-end MYOB reports by end of week 1 of next month at the latest

Stage 1 Action Plan – Foundation

- Calculate BAS and compliance
- Provide month-/quarter-end MYOB file to accountant
- Manage super paperwork, payments and compliance
- Prepare/collate accounts paperwork for bookkeeper
- Manage creditors and debtors
- Liaise with accountant
- Manage WorkCover paperwork and compliance
- Ensure payments to ATO are made on specified dates
- Monitor and manage cash flow.

Marketing

Online lead generation

- SEO company
- PPC – new service provider.

Offline lead generation

- Teleseminars – help identify service providers, transcription services, costs, editing, how-to set-up, prerecord
- Submit articles to magazines and other publications
- Direct marketing
- Speaking engagements – new VA to research and contact potential organisations
- Radio/TV Interviews/Qantas Radio: Talking Business
- Live networking events – VA to check events for selected network groups and schedule in to diary.

Capture leads

- Add new free offer to home page.

In any Foundation business there will be accounts to do, general office admin and marketing foundations to be put in place, and you may want to allocate different aspects of your marketing to resources with different skill sets. A PR expert, for example, may not be your social media guru. Admin may require different skill sets, too, once you break it down.

Once you've created this resource map, a lot of activities will be on it. Don't be overwhelmed! Just do three things with your list:

1. Highlight the priorities.
   - Where are you feeling the most pressure?
   - What does the business need most?

   The answer usually lies in the areas that you just cannot do yourself, and in functions that must be done, like marketing, bookkeeping and accounting.

2. In a different colour, highlight the activities that *you* must do. These activities are where you will add the most value to the business.

3. Create a job description using the above list. Most businesses in Foundation usually need help first with accounts/bookkeeping and marketing support. Whatever your priorities are that you highlighted in (1) above, you now have a job description that you can use to advertise for part-time help or virtual help.

If any of the functions on the above list aren't applicable to your business, just put a line through them for now. Add functions that are relevant to you that may not be on this list.

As your business grows, the functions will also change and grow to include other functions like HR, Sales, Project Management, and more detailed Finance activities.

A virtual team

The easiest, lowest-risk way to start building a team is with virtual resources. These people can work anywhere – around the corner

Stage 1 Action Plan – Foundation

from your home or from an office on the other side of the world – but the one place they don't work is in your office.

As long as you're comfortable using email and Skype, this works really well. Documents and the status of projects can be uploaded to document-sharing sites, and as long as you are clear about your expectations this is a great way to build your first team.

The one caveat I would have is that it works *better* if you choose to work with someone in a time zone that overlaps at least with your working hours.

For example, one VA (virtual assistant) I worked with for over five years was based in France. She was American so no *parlez français* required! She never started work before 9am so that meant I couldn't communicate with her until later in my day – around 5pm depending on whether it was daylight-saving time. That wasn't an issue for the most part, but it did cause some problems when we had deadlines. If I needed her to set up and be involved when I ran webinars, for example, I would have to do them in my evening because she couldn't be available in my morning.

Working with someone in your own time zone is ideal, but you need to weigh that up against the skills and personality of the people on your shortlist.

Most virtual resources charge on an hourly basis, for blocks of time at a reduced rate, or based on a project fee. Do your research and use the sites below to recruit your support team and compare their rates.

Sources of support

There are local individuals who provide in-person and virtual support. The big directories of support resources are listed below, all of which I have used at some stage. If you've decided you're happy to work in a virtual way using email and Skype, in my experience these sites have the largest databases of resources.

Virtual assistants

- **www.assistu.com** I have employed several VAs using this site, which specialises in virtual assistants, and I recommend it. I love the robustness of its process. You need to provide a detailed overview of your business and goals, your work and management style, and what sort of support you require.

    When your application is submitted to the site, potential candidates can review and decide if they like the sound of the brief/your business/you.

    This screening process is really useful in helping you get down to a shortlist. By that stage, you already know their expertise, fees and similar projects they've worked on. From then it's like a standard recruitment process, but not in person. You can email questions to the candidates, set up a time to interview them over the phone or Skype, and they have the opportunity to ask you questions as well.

    You agree to work on whatever basis you require – ad hoc, by the hour or for a specific project, or you can test the relationship, the person and working in a virtual way, with something small to start.

Other sites offering a vast range of resources:

- **www.upwork.com** This incorporates what was Odesk.com and Elance.com. The people available to help you are literally from every part of the world and have all degrees of experience. The site allows past clients to provide feedback and ratings, so you can assess the capabilities and reliability of someone before you contact them. It also shows their fees and how much they have earned from the site, which gives you an indication of how many clients they've had and projects they've worked on.

- **www.fiverr.com** You can find a world of resources to do anything from design, copywriting and video production, to all sorts of quirky and specific services. The going rate for a basic brief is US$5 and it increases from there in US$5 increments depending on the customisation and variation you require. You place an order and pay for it – and you can discuss the brief with your service provider first before deciding to order – and payment is only transferred when you accept the completed order.

Local sites

- **Universities** – a great source of talent, depending on your project. I've recruited a first-class honours graduate to create a lot of marketing content. She worked in our office and from her home and was diligent, reliable and very good. I used the university website which has a student recruitment section. The process is structured here too, which benefits both employer and student.

- **www.99designs.com.au** – the best for design resources. It's a great system, easy to use, and gives you access to a huge database of talent. Although 99 Designs was started in Australia, as with the other resource sites it has individuals and firms located all around the world.

  I've posted many small design projects onto this site. It works a bit differently in that you post your brief onto the site, with the fee you will pay for it, and interested designers then bid for the project. They will present their initial designs so you often have multiple designs to choose from. They may present more than one design.

  When you've awarded the job to a particular designer, they will then submit variations of their design until you're happy with the final submission. Then you confirm the final design, and pay them. Your payment goes into escrow and is released to the designer when they have sent you all the final files.

- **www.lifestylecareers.com.au** – lots of people who are taking time out of traditional corporate roles can be found on this site, from project managers to software developers to recruiters to marketers.

  I recruited an MBA graduate to do some PR and specific marketing activities, as well as organise speaking engagements. She happened to be local, so we had the occasional update meeting over coffee. She was a great resource and delivered the results I required. She had previously had a corporate career and took time off while her children were young.

With all these resources available at bargain rates through to standard hourly rates, there is no reason why you cannot help your Foundation business get off the ground with more support. Depending on your business model and your cash flow, you may be able to grow with full-time resources from the outset. However, for most small businesses, support initially is based on external or contracted resources, casual staff and part-time staff.

Your business will be ready to add new full-time staff when your revenue is at a level that can pay for salaries, superannuation and other associated expenses of employing people – more work space, IT requirements, etc. – on a monthly basis. If you struggle with doing these sorts of cash-flow projections or you've never done one before, have your accountant teach you how to do it.

Chapter worksheets

- Identify your Mastery: www.jennystilwell.com.au/sbceo/mastery
- Marketing Collateral list: www.jennystilwell.com.au/sbceo/collateral

- Choose your Best-Fit Marketing Activities: www.jennystilwell.com.au/sbceo/marketingactivity
- Create Content: www.jennystilwell.com.au/sbceo/contentlist
- Pull it all together with a Marketing Calendar: www.jennystilwell.com.au/sbceo/marketingcalendar

Find these worksheets and tools when you go to the Small Business CEO page on the website: www.jennystilwell.com.au/sbceo.

Chapter highlights

- The key components of your marketing foundations:

    Mastery – how does your business deliver great value to your customers?

    Market – who is your target market; who is your ideal customer?

    Message – what is your value proposition to communicate to your target market?

    Best-fit marketing – choose the marketing mix that works best.

    Marketing system – create a marketing calendar and get someone to implement it for you.
- To manage cash flow, you need to understand sales revenue, margins, fee structures and options, and terms.
- Know where you need help, and how to find the right resources.

CHAPTER 5

Stage 2 – Build Structure

REACHING this stage means your small business is well on the way to becoming a big business, if you get this right! Stage 2 represents the growth of a business to the point that it has become self-sustainable in terms of a repeat client base, with potential new business coming in the door on a regular basis either through sales and marketing activities, referrals, your sales and distribution channels or a combination of any or all of these. There is a team in place which may be small or large depending on how rapidly the business is growing, and it's starting to make money.

Stage 2 is a huge shift for the business owner and is probably the most important stage in putting in the necessary structure and systems to support the business. It is at this stage that the game changes. The person or people who started the business are no longer the only ones in it and no longer do everything. They need to delegate to others, plan ahead and grow their own roles in order to move through this stage.

Dealing with the complexity that comes with this stage is a huge learning curve for most business owners who have never been in a situation like 'the Stage 2 business' before.

A lot of the knowledge of how things work and are meant to work is in the head of the owner. Often, when things 'overheat' to the point where there is too much going on at once, the solution is to throw more resources at the problem. Hence the complexity continues to grow and more resources are not the answer. Spreading the knowledge from the owner to the team *is* part of the answer, and streamlining complexity is the other part of the answer for more structure in your organisation.

Many business owners run the risk of loss of control when they approach Stage 2. Some fail to really understand the importance of building structure, and continue to focus on more growth and the irresistible desire to take all opportunities that are presented. If you neglect structure your business will fail. It is essential to take stock and build structure at this stage, so you can continue on your growth path.

The approach to Build Structure is somewhat prescriptive, but it won't flow smoothly because in most cases the small business CEO has never been a CEO before and is venturing into new and unfamiliar territory. It will take trial and error and time to get through this stage.

Who is in Build Structure?

- Companies (both small and new or large and established) that have been through a relatively fast growth phase and have lots of new clients and work, but are feeling a little out of control with all the growth.
- Any organisation where mistakes and problems are occurring too frequently.
- Any business with a team of people, and the owner is the only one who really knows how things need to be done.

Stage 2 – Build Structure

- A business where the owner is overwhelmed and exhausted by trying to keep it all together.
- A business that isn't performing as well as it could – due to reasons that may be known or may be unclear.

Businesses can move slowly or quickly into Stage 2. Those that experience rapid growth and need to increase their headcount and their overheads will typically find this stage stressful. The reason is that the business owner, who is used to doing pretty much everything in the business on their own, has not learned to delegate or to make a shift with their role from operational to more strategic.

At its worst, Stage 2 can be chaotic and exhausting for the business owner and stressful for employees. It can also be frustrating for customers once it gets to the point where product and service delivery are affected.

If a business at the stage of Build Structure were a person, it would be an adolescent – contrary, rebellious, uncooperative, perfect one minute, hideous the next, showing glimmers of maturity, but always a challenge to try and manage. Of course the adolescent has no option but to go through this phase to become a mature and responsible adult!

Challenges of Build Structure stage

- Dealing with complexity
- Letting go and stepping up to a CEO role.

Dealing with complexity

When you first start your business, it is about as simple and un-complex as it will ever be. It's (usually) just you. Because it's just you, there can't be too much going on with multiple products and services, account matters, client management issues, strategic partners, multiple distribution channels, customer service issues or other operational matters. Accounts and finances are simple (even though managing cashflow may be a challenge!), and business systems are usually no more than spreadsheets.

As the business grows beyond Stage 1 and into Stage 2, everything starts to ramp up as can be seen in Figure 5.1 below.

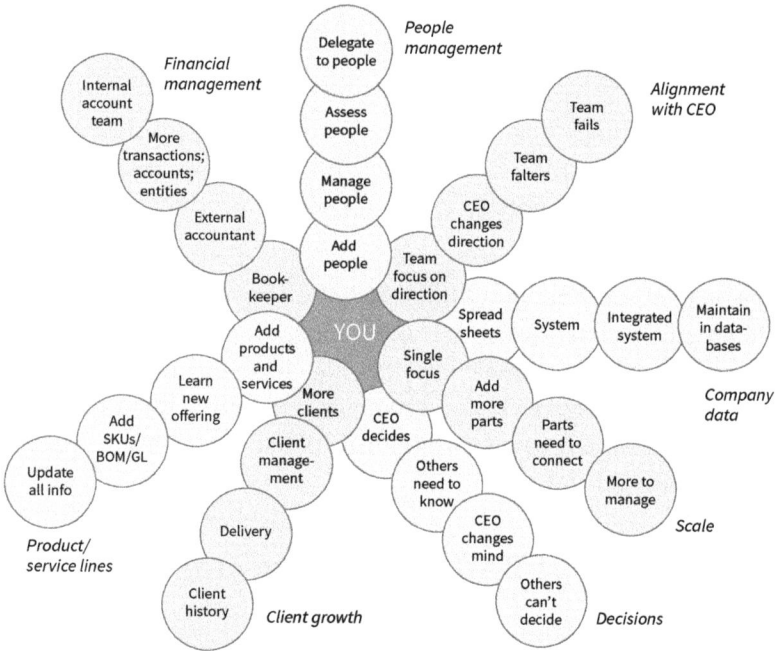

Figure 5.1: Business growth complexity

From a financial management perspective, you may start off with a bookkeeper and an external accountant for compliance, but then the general ledger expands, there are more transactions, more clients, more categories, possibly more entities, different terms for different clients and then you need an internal accounts team to manage all of this.

Initially, company data is held in spreadsheets, which is easy for one person to track accounts receivable, payable and cash flow in linked spreadsheets, as well as track sales performance and client value, product and service price lists and so on.

However, with more users needing access to this data, and more users updating the data, spreadsheets need to be transferred to a system. One day the accounts system needs to be integrated with the operational side of the business especially when you're dealing with stock and inventory. Then maintenance, accuracy and being able to track one entry throughout the entire system is critical.

In terms of developing new products, it's easy when you're in Stage 1 (and easy if you're dealing in services rather than physical products). As your business grows, suddenly the development of new products involves training other members of your team in what they do and their features, benefits, prices; you won't be the only one with new product ideas and as new products are developed and made, this needs to be reflected in the stock keep units, bill of materials and general ledger. Someone needs to maintain this but several people need to be involved in this process. You don't want any of this new data falling through the cracks.

Growth in clients and client management is all part of the added complexity of Stage 2. In the beginning you would have been the only service provider for the most part. Now, you not only have to deal with multiple clients, but also more than one person who actually delivers the service. Are the other people in the team as experienced as you are? Do they deliver the organisation's services in the same way that you do? Are all the company's clients happy and being well managed? Maybe the new members of your team do things better than you and something needs to be changed with regards to how the service is delivered. You will need procedures in place to ensure consistency of service delivery, and in client management.

With regard to decision-making, in the beginning you make the decisions, you act on them, and then you may change your mind and go the other way. When you have a team of people in your business, you need to be mindful that you must communicate your decisions so they know what needs to be done. You also need to communicate any change of decision and explain why (otherwise they lack certainty around what's happening and wonder why you won't tell them what's going on), and eventually, you will need to enable members of your team to make decisions themselves. You cannot continue to make every decision. You must make sure that you and your team are in alignment.

Managing people is a huge challenge for business owners in all stages, but *particularly* in Stage 2. Employing a virtual team is easy because they work in their own space and you are not tied to any ongoing employment commitment. Recruiting your first full-time employee is a huge step for any business, as this person is usually the one who picks up most of the administrative and operational tasks that you don't want to do. They pick up a big load. You will work closely with them. After that, as you continue to add new team members, you will need to manage them, assess them and delegate responsibilities to them. You will need to let go. They will require clarity around their role and your expectations. This can be an extraordinarily stressful time for most business owners who are struggling with all of these challenges at Stage 2.

You started your business with a single focus, then you added more parts, and those parts need to eventually connect and the result is far more to be managed.

You now have to communicate, engage, discuss with your team, delegate, track performance, track delivery, track profit, work with clients, deal with people issues, deal with external suppliers, identify problems, solve problems, manage risk, and make sure everything is running smoothly.

Complexity can overwhelm you. This is when you become tethered by your business, unless you let go and step up. Managing all of this complexity requires a different approach and focus than you have as a Foundation business owner. This is where you need to shift into CEO mode to manage and guide your growing company strategically.

Making the shift to CEO

This doesn't mean changing the title on your business card just for the sake of being a CEO. It means that you step up and acknowledge that you are the leader of a team now. They need your guidance and direction.

I've seen many business owners falter at this stage because of three typical approaches.

One approach is that they throw resources at complexity, rather than simplify complexity. They end up with more people than they really need (and often the wrong people) and still have complexity. Ultimately they are the ones who still have to address a lot of the problems and see their team as mostly ineffectual. Frequently when they do employ more people, they bring in people who are inexperienced, people who won't cost too much, and essentially, people who can be controlled by the business owner.

> Complexity can overwhelm you. This is when you become tethered by your business, unless you let go and step up.

The other approach is failure to change their own role because they don't really know what it should be. It's often a role they haven't been in before and rather than venture into it and maybe get it wrong, they stay where they are from lack of confidence.

The third approach is failing to download what's in their head to their team, so everyone knows what's going on, how things should be done, and who needs to be involved in what. Because things are still in their head, they become a bottleneck because they haven't properly defined roles and delegated accordingly amongst their team.

Not surprisingly, none of these approaches work!

Keys to success in Stage 2

- **Be objective and analytical about everything in your business and everything you decide to do**, including your own role and performance. That is the overriding key to success at this stage.
- **Be objective about the people in your team**, to the point where you can make realistic assessments of whether they are still the right person for the role, and for the business. Many owners bring someone on board when the organisation is very small, and retain this person as the business grows into something quite different from what it was when it started. For example, the part-time bookkeeper you employed in the beginning is not the same person who can now manage all the accounts. The admin support person who was your first employee is unlikely to be the operations manager for a much larger established organisation (and they may well not *want* to be, either).
- **Create the right structure for how you manage and lead your company** from this point – this is essential for growth and your own peace of mind.
- **Stop 'doing' for long enough to take a high level look at your business and get your head out of the detail.** You need a different perspective in order to make these adjustments. Failure to do this is *always* a roadblock to continued stable growth.

- **Look at what you do and how you do it, with a view to finetuning and improving it.** As you grow and as your business becomes more complex, your processes must become more streamlined and more robust, and have less of 'you' in them. This requires considerable work from your whole team to map out a better way than the one you have now.

Build Structure examples

CARLA – CONSTRUCTION SERVICES

Carla was extremely driven to succeed, but lacked the skill set to run a growing business and recruit and manage a growing team. Add to that considerable growth in a short period of time, and the mix was classic Stage 2.

The fundamental problem that kept this business firmly entrenched in the complexities of Stage 2 was that Carla was a fierce control freak and refused to let go. She wanted everything done a certain way, but never took the time to set up systems for what her desired way looked like. She didn't trust new employees to get on with the job because she wanted everything done exactly the way she would do it, and so virtually continued to do a lot of their roles herself; she wouldn't let her team put any systems or procedures in place, no matter how small, as she wanted to do that herself; and she failed to grasp the value that new team members could add in their own areas of expertise.

Carla was also good at selling her organisation's capabilities, which resulted in winning more and more projects, increasingly with larger companies. These larger organisations were demanding evidence of service and delivery procedures as a standard requirement of doing business.

Carla continued to resist the efforts of her new team to step up and take greater ownership of their respective areas. Fortunately for Carla, her two key people had faith in themselves and the business and persevered. Eventually Carla *had* to let go and yield to the pressure in order to meet the requirements and timelines of their larger clients. It was a tussle between her and her team, but the pressure of a rapidly growing business without structure and systems was the catalyst for change.

I spoke to Carla again while writing this book. She admitted that she couldn't see the importance of a focus on structure at the time, or why I kept advising her to let go, delegate, and engage her team to build the structure that her business so desperately required. With hindsight, she thanked me for my insistence.

She also told me that she had spent six months in another state trying to establish her business there. Again, at the time my advice was 'too fast, too soon' as her business and resources were not ready to be stretched to the limit of their growth capacity. That exercise cost her half her business.

She's taken a few hard hits but her business is now back on track and I think the experience was enlightening for her. That's how we grow and become better CEOs! Carla took the step from business owner to CEO just in time.

DYLAN – SPECIALIST CONSULTING FIRM

Dylan's business made it through Stage 2 by imploding first, then re-emerging as a smaller version of itself.

The organisation grew rapidly and made a lot of money, and Dylan was intent on expanding equally as rapidly. However, because the business had grown so fast, it was outgrowing its original way of operating. It needed new procedures and systems; it was focused on the wrong measures of performance; and no-one really knew how things 'worked' any more as everyone seemed to do things a bit differently.

People were employed too quickly without going through due process; there were too many people, too few processes, and no-one really knew quite what was going on, so a lot of people reverted to working on their own rather than as part of the team.

Dylan set a frantic pace and drove everyone incredibly hard to bring in more business. Not enough time was being spent on managing the business and nurturing client relationships, and no-one was looking at the real results the organisation was getting. Dylan equated more jobs with more money, but it didn't equate to a stable or viable business.

Dylan had no management experience and it was showing. He thought he was a leader, but he was a good salesperson when he was left to develop business on his own. Acquiring new clients was the primary focus, but because the pace was so frantic and everyone was being driven so hard, important things were falling through the cracks. Not enough time was being spent on nurturing client relationships. *The average value of their top tier clients fell by more than 60%;* the new clients they were bringing on board were worth smaller and smaller amounts to the business. They were bringing in the wrong types of clients – quantity over quality – and neglecting the right clients, who were their existing clients.

Dylan did a lot of things really well, which was why this business grew in the first place. He cared enough about the business to get external advice when things were becoming too overwhelming. The main thing he failed to do at this crucial stage was to put the necessary structure into the business by way of the right team with clear roles and accountabilities, streamlining and standardising core processes to improve consistency of delivery across the consulting team, and taking the time to do that properly before allowing more growth to occur.

Dylan enjoyed the chase of the next sale and was always too busy to spend time analysing the business. He failed to step up as the organisation's CEO and also failed to pay attention to increasing overheads, a directionless team, declining client value and unnecessary overspending within the business.

Eventually the business imploded and Dylan was forced to strip it back – people, offices, some clients. He scaled down considerably but never addressed complexity and lack of structure and systems, merely removed them. There is every possibility that something similar could happen second time around, if the business starts to grow again without addressing these fundamental structural issues.

ADAM – BUSINESS TO BUSINESS SERVICES

This organisation built structure just in the nick of time, and from there moved strategically and confidently into Stage 3. The only reason this was able to happen was because Adam was able to let go and shift his role to that of CEO.

As often happens, the first operational employee grows with the company and their role grows to a level that is too big for them. Admin support people become 'office managers' or 'business managers', technical or support people are elevated after a few years of the organisation's growth to 'operations managers'. People are elevated to roles they are ill-equipped for. They lack the experience, the skills and sometimes the desire to take on a role that becomes vastly different from their earlier role with the organisation.

When there's a friendship connection and a sense of loyalty, business owners never let these people go and often let them flounder in the role when it's obviously too big for them.

I have seen so many business owners promote a junior person to a senior role, because the organisation is growing and needs more support. What they fail to see, often through a sense of loyalty or failing to be objective about the situation, is that what the company really needs is a new person with far more experience.

That happened in this organisation. The operations manager, who had begun as a general assistant in the business when it started, kept everything to herself and failed to communicate with the rest of the team when there were problems. She was trying to cover up the fact that she could no longer do the role. It was too big for her.

This led to all sorts of ongoing problems in the business with low morale, a lot of complexity that had never been streamlined, firefighting on an almost daily basis, and an exhausted and frustrated business owner.

Adam knew he had to make some changes. After a thorough review of the business, the structure of the organisation was changed. Adam shifted his role to managing director, let the necessary people go, and brought in an experienced person to run the day-to-day operations of the organisation.

Procedures were put in place to simplify and structure operations; roles and accountabilities were clarified; and a strategic plan was developed that provided a roadmap for the team to grow the business in a strategic way.

Over time, Adam was able to develop new business opportunities for ongoing growth, knowing that a capable team and the right reporting and accountability structure would enable him to stay on top of his company's performance.

BEN – MARKETING SERVICES BUSINESS

Ben was an outgoing and confident marketing expert. He practised what he preached and was able to acquire his own clients as well as delivering successful marketing campaigns for his clients.

His strength was almost his downfall. He was good at growing his business, and acquired a sizeable client base in a few short years. He was decisive, usually based on gut feeling with little strategic thought. He grew quickly, but in an unstructured way, and soon had a large team of people servicing the clients, none of whom contributed to the management, administrative or operational side of the business. That was *all* left to Ben, who also delivered the service for the organisation's largest clients.

He had limited management experience, so he found himself in a situation he was ill-equipped to manage, which gave him a lot of stress. But he didn't want to let go. The load became too heavy. He was the head rainmaker bringing in all the business, he was recruiting and managing his team and briefing them on what their clients wanted, he was coping with all of the administrative and operational side of the business, and he was still the primary account manager for some key accounts.

Ben failed to develop core procedures for how they delivered their services for clients, resulting in inconsistent results depending on which marketers were engaged for client projects. Some client dissatisfaction crept in; their previously high success rate for clients started to slide.

Ben had placed himself under pressure because he refused to delegate anything to his team and was stretched across all aspects of growing and managing his business, including servicing his clients.

Not surprisingly, the lack of structure at this stage of growth was too much. He transformed his business by downsizing as far as he could – no more office, no more team, fewer clients and time out. Then when he'd had enough time out to think about what he really enjoyed doing, he started again, by himself. He is now in Foundation and, without the initial complexity of Stage 2, has reclaimed control of his business and his happiness.

Sometimes growth for growth's sake isn't the right strategy.

Top 3 strategies to use in Stage 2

1. Identify core business functions and resource gaps for your organisation's structure.
2. Get the right team in place and get everyone clear on responsibilities and expectations – for their roles and yours.
3. Map out and improve your core organisation processes.

Stage 2 occurs for every new business on the verge of its next phase of expansion, and it also occurs in established businesses that have been through growth and need to take stock, consolidate and shore up their structure to make sure the core business is well supported.

Once a business has become viable, it will continue on a journey passing backwards and forwards between Stage 2 and Stage 3 for some years. This is a natural and necessary occurrence, as business expansion will always necessitate some adjustment and correction to the organisation's structure.

Chapter highlights

- Growth for the sake of growing isn't always the right strategy.
- Stage 2 is where the business owner needs to shift from being a doer in the business to being the leader of the business.
- Becoming the CEO leading the business can only be done when you delegate to your team and allow them to help you implement the necessary structure for continued viability and growth.
- Stage 2 brings increasing complexity along with growth. This complexity needs to be managed so the business can continue to grow profitably.

CHAPTER 6

Stage 2 Action Plan – Build Structure

STAGE 2 is a really exciting time for a business as it grows, and can also be one of the most stressful! Many business owners insist on retaining their original role and want to be involved in everything else as well. This is potentially the downfall of Stage 2 businesses. Others hang on to their multifaceted original role but also place a heavy reliance on the first support person they employed. This person is typically an admin assistant, a bookkeeper or a marketing support person.

As the business grows, the owner places more and more reliance on this support person, to the extent that a bookkeeper may become involved in admin tasks, as may an online marketing support person. It's not uncommon for admin assistants to eventually become office or business managers. Sometimes this works, but mostly it doesn't.

With an inexperienced team, the competency gap between the owner of the organisation and the next level down is way too big.

The owner still has to step in and make decisions and solve problems, because the team lacks the skills and experience to take charge. It is for this very reason that many business owners lament the growth of their team 'I don't know why I employ all these people when I have to do most of it myself...'

You can usually identify a company trying to deal with the complexities of Stage 2 if you happen to be a customer. They tend to get orders wrong, they are incredibly slow to follow up with their accounts, you may deal with different people for the same inquiry and not really know the role of the person you're dealing with (is it the right person to talk to?), and they will often run short on stock. It's because they lack structure.

Let's launch into the action plan for Stage 2, with the top priorities to focus on being:

- Company organisation structure – how you organise your team to support you
- People – right people and clear roles
- Processes – get core processes out of your head.

Each of these has several parts.

Establish organisation structure – identify core functions

In order to map out your organisation structure, you need to identify the core functions in your business. When you do this exercise, do not put employee names against these functions. Just focus on what functions the business needs in order to run smoothly.

These will depend on the type of business you have and its geographic reach, but typically, the core functions will be a configuration of some of the following. We touched on functions

Stage 2 Action Plan – Build Structure

in Foundation. On this checklist tick those functions you have in your business now, and highlight those that you think you will need (and add any others if they aren't on this list but are relevant to your business):

- Accounts payable
- Accounts receivable
- Invoicing
- Compliance (BAS and annual returns)
- Finance and admin
- Sales/new business development
- Marketing
- Account management
- Operations
- Human resources
- Warehouse
- Brand management
- Product development
- Planning and scheduling
- Project management
- Customer service
- Technical support
- Purchasing
- Office management
- Installation/service delivery
- Production
- Quality assurance
- IT support
- Etc...

When you've identified the core functions in your business, put them together into logical groups. For example, of the roles highlighted above, they would be grouped logically together like this:

Finance and admin

- Purchasing
- Accounts payable
- Accounts receivable
- Invoicing
- Compliance
- Office management.

Operations

- Warehouse
- Planning and scheduling
- Project management
- Technical support
- Installation/service delivery
- Production
- IT support.

Sales and marketing

- Brand management
- Product development
- Project management
- Customer service
- New business development
- Account management.

Other functions

Depending on your business, you may put *Customer Service* under operations, or under Sales and Marketing, or as a function that reports directly to you. It needs to be an independent function. What this means is, when you have customer service issues, for example with product faults, you don't necessarily want the person who has overall responsibility for product development to also manage issues with the product. It can present a conflict of interest and is best separated. It really depends on the business size, the people in charge and their capabilities and experience, and what the CEO considers to be of the most importance. The most important roles report to the CEO.

Human resources is not usually a core function until a company is large enough to warrant a full-time team. Many business owners give this function to whoever heads up Finance and Admin, but this isn't often the best person to manage it. It is a better idea to have an external HR resource you can call on to assist with performance management, employee problems, individual coaching, employee agreements, due process, compliance and other necessary legal requirements when you have a team of people working for you.

Quality assurance is another function that needs to be independent. Faulty product, being reported in to the person in charge of producing the product, may present conflict. If the CEO places a high value on quality, this function may report directly to the CEO.

There is no science to creating your organisation structure, but there are guidelines that help and considerations you need to be mindful of, such as these.

When you first start to grow your team you will have a few people to manage only, but defining who is responsible for what, and letting them get on with it, is the first step for you as the CEO to step up and back.

People

Map out your organisation structure

Typically, as you start to grow your team, you end up with many direct reports (see Figure 6.1). As new people come on, they all report to you, either because there's no-one else to report to and not enough people for the structure you need, or because you prefer to know exactly what they're doing and direct their activity. You have a team, but you are still involved in the day-to-day running of the business and can't see anything but the detail of daily operations.

Figure 6.1: Example organisational chart

From Business Owner...

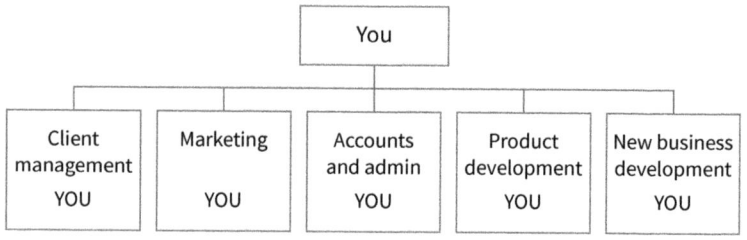

This is where you become overwhelmed and somewhat anxious, because now you are employing people, and they are adding considerable cost to your organisation's overheads, but you still feel you need to be involved in everything your team is doing.

Your goal is to move to a position where you have a few direct reports, who manage the rest of the team, which represents a much better organised business (see Figure 6.2).

The top three functions that can take all the load from the CEO are Finance and Administration, Sales and Marketing, and Operations. Underneath these broad functions you could have hundreds of people or just a few.

Stage 2 Action Plan – Build Structure

Figure 6.2: Example of a more mature company structure

To CEO

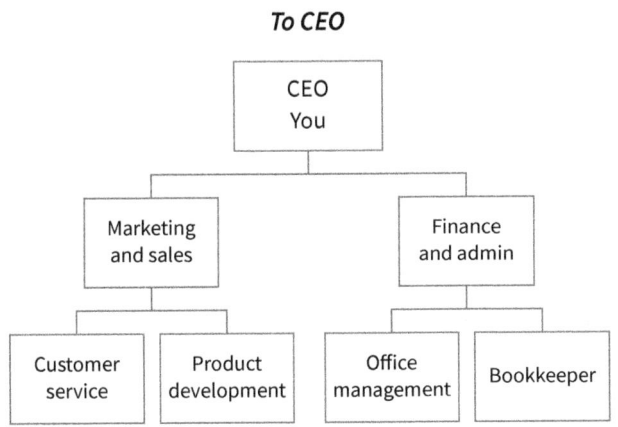

When you have a large company, the heads of these functions may have titles like 'General Manager' or 'Director'. When you have a small organisation, these roles may have small titles, like 'Sales and Marketing Coordinator' or 'Bookkeeper'. By keeping the titles small, it gives you scope to grow the people and/or the roles, and it doesn't necessarily follow that the people with small roles and small titles will be the same people with big roles and big titles once you have a bigger organisation.

I'm repeating this point because it's important to leave room for change and new people in the future. Don't trap yourself with the wrong people who don't have the capabilities once your company grows. Right now, your only objective as the CEO is to get support, be able to delegate, start building a structure on which you can grow further, and step back and focus on your own role.

As the CEO you do not want everyone reporting to you. It's fine if you have two employees but even if you have 10 or 15, you need them to be organised in a way (and capable enough) that not everything needs to be run by you.

At one point in my career I had 18 direct reports, which is completely untenable, and it wasn't until I was able to make changes to the ownership of the company that I could simplify the organisation structure to a core team of about six people who reported to me.

When you minimise your direct reports as far as possible, reducing them to only those people who are responsible for your core functional areas of the business, your role has completely shifted to that of the CEO. Ideally, you want no more than five to seven direct reports, and less if you have a small business or one with a simple model.

Get clear on responsibilities and expectations

Defining roles, responsibilities and expectations, and how each role or function relates to others on the organisation chart, will support your business as you scale up. Everyone needs clarity on what they have to do, who they report to, and what is expected of them. Your team will have to communicate and work together on your core processes, and have clear communication and reporting lines for what outcomes they are all working to.

I strongly suggest that before you create Position Descriptions for your team, you draw an organisation chart with functions and roles that you think you will need in the future as you grow. Do NOT put in anyone's name, just the job function that will be needed within your organisation.

When you have spent some time future-gazing, be honest and place the team you currently have in roles that match their skills and capabilities. This is a useful exercise as a litmus test for the resources you need and the resources you have, and where your support is going to come from. Remember to focus first on roles, and then place people into those roles. Don't focus on the people you have and put them into roles that they can't fill, just because they are the only resources you have right now.

Stage 2 Action Plan – Build Structure

What often happens with early Stage 2 companies is that the wrong person goes into the wrong role. A junior person is often given a senior role because they are the only one performing a core function.

> A junior person is often given a senior role because they are the only one performing a core function.

For example, an organisation may have a junior brand manager who also does some general marketing functions. They make that person 'Marketing Manager' or sometimes because it sounds better to the national clients, 'National Marketing Manager'. There are two fundamental problems with this:

- When the company grows further to the point they really need an experienced person to head up Marketing on a national basis, that person will not have the experience for the role and will need to report to the new more experienced person. You've given them a title that is way bigger than the scope of their capabilities, and it doesn't reflect the role that they are really doing.
- The less experienced person is likely to leave the organisation, being disillusioned and unhappy.

This happens all the time. You have to give people the roles and responsibilities they're qualified and experienced to do. If you give an inexperienced person a big title, guaranteed as long as the organisation continues to grow, they won't be the person doing the big job in the future.

Don't think you can avoid employing more experienced – and more expensive – people to join your team. The value they add will far outweigh the cost to the business.

Create Position Descriptions for everyone

Position Descriptions will ideally include:

- Title of the role

- Purpose of the role
- Who the role reports to
- Who the role is responsible for (i.e. other roles or a department)
- Key responsibilities
- Expenditure authorisation and up to what amount
- How the role will be assessed (key performance indicators).

(You can download a Position Description template from my website with the link at the end of this chapter.)

If it's an existing role and the existing employee is staying in that role, have them make a list of their responsibilities.

If it's a new role, you can do one of two things:

- If you're employing a new person to help an existing person, have the existing person make a list of everything the new person can/will help them with. You can edit it if need be.
- If there are things that aren't getting done, or things that you no longer want to have to do, write out a list of those things. That will be the basis of your Position Description.

You can always search online for sample descriptions for similar roles, and look at recruitment ads for similar roles. The key responsibilities will be itemised. It's a good reference check and makes the process easier and faster.

Create your new Position Description as CEO

Be ruthless and delegate anything that is not the best use of your time or talents. Always ask yourself:

'What is it that I need to do in order to maximise the value I can add to the organisation?'

You need to take a bigger picture perspective now. If everyone knows what they're meant to do in their role, and what is expected of them, they should be able to get on with things. Yes, they will have problems and challenges and need your help, but you also need to train them to think through the problem and come up with their own possible solutions, before they come and see you. Train your team with this classic management practice: 'Don't bring me a problem, bring me your solution.'

Of course there will be times, and many times if they're inexperienced, when they just don't know, but at least they will learn to think the situation through before they bring it to you.

As the CEO, you should be focused on leadership. You need to provide direction, strategic focus, think about innovation to give you a competitive edge and add more value to your clients, build relationships with key clients and suppliers, and regularly monitor the controls and levers in your business so you know exactly what's happening. You always need to make sure you have the right people in the right roles, and you need to focus on growth and the future.

If you aren't focused on these things, who is?

Establish key performance indicators (KPIs)

These take time as you really need to think about quantitative and qualitative measures for what the role entails.

Quantitative performance indicators for different roles could be things like:

- Sales per month/quarter/year
- Leads per month/quarter/year
- New clients acquired
- Margin
- Customer retention
- Stock turns

- Products sold by type
- Quality pass rates
- Average value of client projects
- Zero litigation or fines due to statutory non-compliance
- Timely management of payments and receipts to produce positive cashflow
- Accuracy in, and timely delivery of, financial management reports
- Brand margins
- Number of new ranges taken up by retailers.

Qualitative performance requirements are subjective, so a way to assess them must be possible, for example:

- Contribution to management meetings each month (assess by attendance; assess by ideas/solutions submitted that may be recorded in meeting minutes)
- Assist in induction of new employees (get feedback from new employees on how helpful the process/person was in explaining things; was the person involved in helping to induct all new employees?)
- Effective recruitment and training of office administration staff to reduce need for involvement of/reliance on CEO
- Contribution toward achievement of overall organisation goals
- Cooperation and support provided to all members of the company
- Attendance and participation in meetings, and consistent follow through on allocated actions
- Provision of support to business development team as required

- Contribution toward achievement of overall marketing and sales goals
- Cooperation and support provided to all members of the organisation.

Each Position Description should have both qualitative and quantitative measures as one measures attitude and behaviour and the other measures results.

Incentives and rewards

Building a good team is definitely one of the big challenges in growing any business. Finding good people isn't easy, having a cultural fit with your business is important, and once you find good people you want to keep them!

When the business owner is at the stage where they have started to delegate and let go, they will also have started to feel the relief and freedom that comes with that. And so it is around this time that thoughts turn to rewards and incentives to secure their key people.

Equity

Many business owners want to offer employees equity in their business. They do this in the belief that it will secure loyalty and tenure. Giving an employee a share of your business *seems* like a great idea – lock them in, make them feel good with the reward you're giving them, and when you sell there will be plenty to go around for you and for their small share.

Most people who are given a small percentage of the company in equity don't really understand what that means. Certainly not the ones I've asked over the years. Those who have been given a token amount to secure their loyalty don't have shareholder agreements, so there's nothing in writing to verify exactly what it is they do have claim to. And that doesn't stop them from leaving.

The cost of the legal fees to put in place a shareholder agreement for a nominal shareholder is not really worth it unless you intend to make good on the agreement with something tangible. For example, when you give someone, say, 5% equity in your company, it's a loose end without a shareholder agreement. If you sold your business for $10 million and had to pay out $500,000 to someone because you gifted them 5% 20 years before, how would you feel? Has that person been a driving force in helping get your company to that point, or not? If they have, then that equity share has been well worth it.

These are the most common drawbacks to this strategy:

- when your employees don't want a little piece of your organisation
- when they want to go and then you have to deal with the little share you've given them
- they didn't particularly want it in the first place, so are not likely to be motivated to deliver more value
- when an agreement is not in place, so your 'reward' is intangible.

There are situations when this is the right strategy in the context of the bigger plan you have for your business, and your own exit. Sometimes there is an exceptional person or two who will be there with you on the journey through to the completion of Stage 4. Mostly, it's been my experience that there are better ways to reward.

Bonus

If you want to reward key people, or any members of your team for that matter, and you decide to give bonuses, make sure they are tied to specific outcomes.

If you hand out random bonuses because you've had a good year, or because it's Christmas, without explaining to your team why you're doing it, you set up expectation. They will expect the same next year – just because it's Christmas!

A better strategy, which gives value to the company and the individual employee, is to tie the bonus to the achievement of a specific goal or outcome. For example, you may have someone in your team project-manage a relocation of your business from one office to another. If this is done by a certain date without missing any client or delivery deadlines, you may choose to provide a once-off bonus to that employee for achieving something specific over and above their regular responsibilities.

This kind of bonus doesn't need to be repeated but can be tied to deliverables that benefit both the company and the employee who receives the bonus for achieving the desired outcome.

If you commit to bonuses ahead of time, you need to make sure that the company's performance will be such that bonus payments can be made.

Profit share

My preferred form of incentive and reward is profit share. It needs to be set up so that the share of profit that is allocated to bonuses is a percentage of profit, not a dollar amount, and communicated clearly to your team. These are my reasons:

- You will always retain a set percentage of the profit regardless of the dollar amount. For example, you allocate 20% of your profit to bonuses and retain 80%.
- The better the organisation performs, the greater the share allocated for employee bonus payments, but you don't need to allocate bonuses if the organisation doesn't make any profit.
- Individual percentages of this profit-share bonus are based on each person's performance, so if they don't perform they don't receive a bonus.

- Everyone understands that the better their contribution, the more likely the business will perform well and reward them in return.
- There is no sense of entitlement like there can be with random and unspecified bonuses. Your employees will understand exactly how this works and what needs to happen for everyone to be rewarded.

On the bus or off the bus

If you're the driver of your own organisation, and your team is all on the bus with you – on the journey with you – you need to be certain you aren't carrying any underperforming passengers.

Getting the right people into the right role for the organisation is a combination of intuition and also following a specific process to identify what you need for the role, as well as what you need for a cultural fit, and making that clear when you recruit and interview for the role.

There are questions to ask as a guideline when you're trying to decide if you have the right person in the right role.

The role

Always ask: if you removed the incumbent person from the role, would you be inclined to change the role in any way? For example, you may find you have a long-standing person (maybe your first employee) in a role. The person and the role become inextricably entwined. Once you start to think about the role on its own, it frees up your thinking to design the role in a way that works best for the business as it is now (not as it was before).

The person

Always ask two questions:

1. If you didn't have a specific role for this person, would you

still want them to be in your business somewhere? If the answer is 'yes' then you have someone who is bound to add value once you match their capabilities with a function that would help grow your business.
2. Would I have employed this person, if I knew at the time what I now know about them/their performance/abilities? If the answer is 'no' then you need to seriously re-evaluate the position with this employee.

Letting people go is always extremely difficult. It's a horrible task that most business owners and CEOs put off for too long. You can use this rule of thumb to identify who needs to get off the bus. Figure 6.3 below illustrates this point by considering the how much time you spend managing certain groups of staff and how that correlates with achieving results.

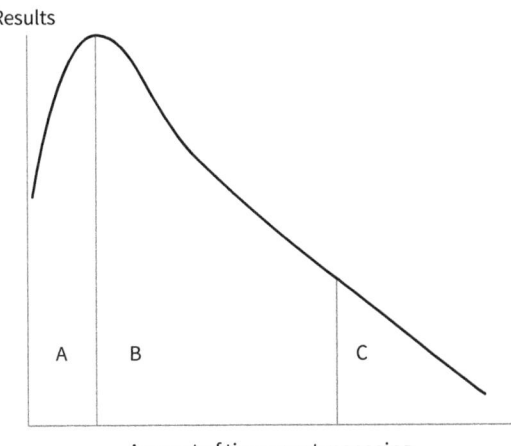

Figure 6.3: Management time vs results

A-people

A-people do more than their share in the organisation. They get the results and you spend the least amount of time managing them, because they don't need it. They're motivated and they take initiative and they get their job done. They are the stars.

C-people

C-people produce the least and take up most of your management time. They may resist, complain, procrastinate, make mistakes, hide their lack of progress and challenge everything they're asked to do. At the worst they can be poisonous in criticising the business, you, and anyone else, and ultimately turning other employees against you and the business. They slow you down and suck the life out of you.

B-people

B-people form the bulk of the rest of your team. In most cases they won't suddenly become your stars – unless you've had them in the wrong roles and you change that – but also they won't become your Cs, either.

Get your C-people out as fast as possible. If you find any of your Bs are getting too close to the C end of the curve in terms of their contribution or their attitude, you will need to try and performance-manage them to lift their game.

Example – a challenging C-person

One client had let a C-person stay on the bus for far too long. This person had been with the business for a long time and knew a lot about the organisation's clients and internal procedures. He also knew his subject matter well. But he challenged everything to the point where he simply would refuse to implement and refuse to act on things he'd been asked to do. His passive-aggressive behaviour was creating enormous tension between him, the managing director and other senior consultants.

The owner of the business was sure that the other people in the business wouldn't be able to carry the load if this person were to leave. I managed to convince him that the fresh energy in the business once the C-person left would be positive for the rest of the team. We performance-managed him out – it wasn't easy – and the impact was instant. The rest of the team were so relieved that he had gone, they didn't mind taking on his workload until we'd found a replacement.

> Never be scared to get the C-people off the bus. They don't belong on your journey.

Processes

You can have processes – systems – for everything in your business. The best businesses do. In the case of entrepreneurial businesses in Stage 2, the most important processes that should be mapped out are those that form the backbone of your core activity. They could be how you provide your service or develop your products and brands, or how your supply chain works.

The Gating Process™

A system I developed for my clients is the Gating Process™, where each key step has a number of prerequisites for the new product to pass through the next 'gate'. It could be used for any process in the organisation requiring authorisation at different points, or involving different people throughout the process.

I worked with a client in the fast-moving consumer goods (FMCG) market, where the 'F' was their mode of operation. They moved quickly with many projects on the go at once, developing whole ranges across multiple private-label and their own brands. As a result, the complexity in the business was considerable.

At one point in their growth they began to suffer from delays and bottlenecks when the CEO was travelling or in meetings, as no-one was authorised to make approvals or decisions in his absence. In addition, no-one had the overall map of how new products were created from the start of the process through the supply chain and to delivery into customer stores. Things could be missed if the CEO wasn't across every step in the process.

This situation is typical for a small company where the founder knows each step of the process and makes all the decisions. Over time a team is employed and each new person has their role to perform, with the CEO still holding all the controls.

Part of the stepping-up process is when the CEO is able to see the value in empowering the right people in the team to be responsible for certain decisions on their own, as backup for when the CEO isn't available, or in conjunction with the CEO as a double-check point.

We worked through the Gating Process™ to map out everything that happened, or needed to happen, and the approval gates that the process had to go through. There were key points where decisions had to be made to continue with new product ideas, or stop, and to approve spending at different stages, or not.

Not only did this exercise streamline the new product development process, but it gave everyone in the team an appreciation of other departments and individual roles, and their part in the overall process. Everyone had a new understanding of the need for communication!

Figure 6.4 below is an example of the overall process. Each step in the process had its own sub-process so any new person to the organisation could learn this, and understand exactly how the company operated for their core process.

This process is how you start to build real structure into your organisation and start relieving the pressure on you.

Stage 2 Action Plan – Build Structure

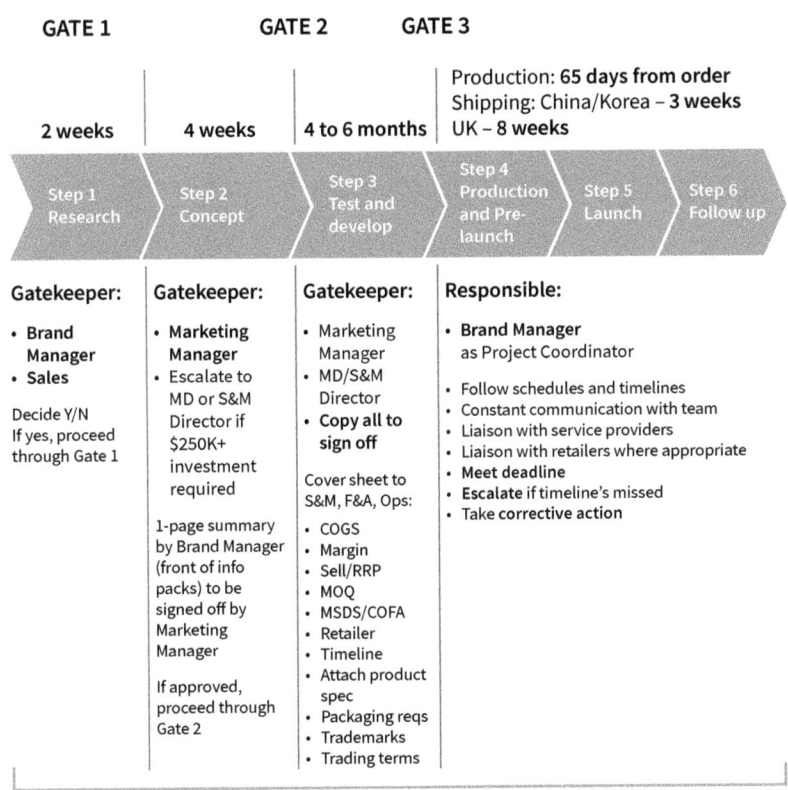

Figure 6.4: New product development process – gates and timeline overview (example)

Concept to launch/in-store = 8 to 11 months

The important thing is not to try to do an operations manual for every single process in your business. Unless you're trying to achieve ISO certification you won't need it, because you won't follow every single process. Just start with the core thing that your business does and map out your end-to-end process for that. You may map out:

- how client projects are delivered from start to finish and handed off to different people at different points

- how new products are developed within your organisation
- how your costing and pricing process works for client projects from start to finish, including calculating all costs, calculating and setting fees, and approval of fees and margins
- how your tender-submission process works
- how your quality-control process works if you have a production facility.

Your process may simply be a sequence of events that need to be adhered to in a strict sequence – for example, painters, car-wash attendants and gardeners who have systemised their process to reduce time and cost use a particular sequence and technique, so anyone new could step in and get into the flow.

If your business makes something for customers or provides a core service to clients, you will benefit from mapping out how you do it. The Gating Process™ achieves a number of things:

- It helps familiarise new people with the organisation's core processes quickly and easily.
- It reinforces who can authorise what.
- It gets the 'how' out of individual heads and into the DNA of the organisation.
- It assists with decision-making, by taking people through the actual steps to reach a yes-no decision on whether to proceed.
- It simplifies complexity.
- It gets your team involved in defining and implementing procedures, and so empowers them to get on with it.
- It helps free the CEO to shift to a more strategic role.

Protection

The third essential part of building structure is protection. This is all about the commercial structure of your business to protect

Stage 2 Action Plan – Build Structure

your assets, limit your liability, protect you against the worst-case scenarios, and achieve compliance from a tax and legal perspective.

If you are a director of your company entity you will have clear and comprehensive responsibilities set out under the *Corporations Act (2001)*. You need to be compliant with these. However, this section contains a high-level summary of key considerations regarding the commercial structure of your business. Commercial structure is *critical*.

Outcomes		Key components
• Protect assets • Limit liability • Protect against worst case • Compliance.		Company structure/entity Contracts and shareholder agreements Terms and conditions Intellectual property Insurances.

I have seen people ignore this component of building structure to their detriment, with some business owners more preoccupied with creating a company procedures manual than getting the commercial structure of their business in place.

Yes, put in place procedures for your core processes that can have the greatest impact if things go wrong, but do not neglect commercial structure. If you do, you're opening the individual owners up to both asset and personal risk. If you own property or other assets you will want to protect them in the event that your business can't meet creditor payments, loan repayments or other liabilities.

I'm not a lawyer, taxation specialist or accountant, so I'll just touch on a couple of these points about protection and recommend that you outsource this to your own legal and financial advisors. Simply ask them what you need to have in place given your business and personal situation and structure, and ask them to advise you on what needs to be done. Delegate the commercial aspects to them while you focus on other things like procedures and people priorities.

Shareholders and equity

Having a shareholders' agreement is like insurance or a prenuptial agreement – it is only there for the worst-case scenario or if there's a sudden change in the relationship between the shareholders. If there is more than one shareholder in a company, you need to have one of these agreements.

The worst situation would be when things become litigious and ugly with irreconcilable differences. A less extreme outcome is that 'what to do next' becomes difficult.

- What if one of the shareholders wants to get out of the business?
- What if one of the shareholders dies?
- What if one of the shareholders acts illegally?
- What if the shareholders have an irreconcilable argument?
- Do you have to give your other partner the first option if one of you wants to opt out at one stage, if one of you wants to sell your share?
- What if something happens to one of you?

Challenging situations can arise when there is more than one shareholder in a business. For example, a partnership may start on equal footing but proceed to the point where one person is primarily responsible for the growth of the organisation and the other has taken a backseat.

- What about the event where one feels that 50% share of a company is not reflective of the value they've put in and the contribution they've made?
- What if that person wants to buy the other out?

- Alternatively, what if the passenger wants to sell? Do they have to offer their share to the other partner first? How will the business be valued?
- If an older shareholder dies, leaving a younger one in charge of running their company, what happens to that person's shares? Do they revert to their family? Does the younger partner have to buy them out? Again, how will the business be valued?

These sorts of questions and situations need to be addressed in the beginning so there is a document to refer back to that reflects the owners' original intentions when everything was working smoothly.

You can find all sorts of shareholder agreement templates online, and if one is relevant to your business structure it's a good starting point to identify the things that you need to be thinking of, and the things that you need to have answers to.

Your lawyer will be able to give you a template as well and then guide you through the process. It is a bit arduous and brings up lots of questions that don't have definitive answers until you think through what would work best for you. It's an important part of your commercial structure.

Contracts

Agreements can be as simple as a one-page document signed by the relevant parties. They can be as complex as *War and Peace*! Here are some fairly standard contracts you would have in place or start putting in place at Stage 2:

- **Employee agreement** – explains what is expected of your employee and their required conduct.
- **Non-disclosure agreement (NDA) or confidentiality agreement** – useful if you're discussing a new idea, venture, product, etc. that you don't want anyone to discuss. It doesn't

stop people from telling others, and if they do it's probably going to be hard to trace, but it does dissuade the 'talkers' from doing so.

- **Supply agreement** – you may have these with some of your key suppliers where product quality and delivery in full and on time are critical components of the relationship. Your customers may ask this of you.
- **Heads of agreement** – used to indicate an intention to do business with another party. If you are considering a large-scale project, joint venture or strategic partnership, you may draw up a heads of agreement to indicate intent and as a precursor to a more detailed contract.
- **Distribution agreement** – where one party is selling or distributing the other's products, an agreement covering territories, sales targets, pricing, supply, delivery and all aspects related to how this will be done, and expectations and exceptions on both sides.

Never sign a contract without going through every line. I've seen contracts where the CEO has signed it without reading all of it or running it past a commercial lawyer, and without being fully aware of the potential exposure they face if delivery clauses aren't met.

Terms and conditions

When you agree to become a supplier of a product or service, you must have clear terms and conditions. It's no good to simply quote a price or a fee and be done with it. You need to be clear about any payments upfront, milestone deliverables when you will invoice for a percentage of the total, interest accumulation if payments aren't made on time, and other conditions that will protect your income.

For example, if your terms say you will invoice in full on completion of delivery – and I hope these are *not* your terms – what if you have a situation where the client won't sign off and

Stage 2 Action Plan – Build Structure

wants variations and adjustments to what you've delivered? It could potentially drag on forever, so you've got to think about the terms and conditions that will close the loop and enable you to not only be paid, but legally be entitled to payment if the client is trying to avoid paying you.

It needs to be clear when you engage in a business relationship with someone that they understand the expectations and the responsibilities around payment terms. You need to also consider warranties, returns and refunds, and liability if something goes wrong. For example, if you use a subcontractor to do a renovation project, and something of the client's is damaged, who is liable for the expense to repair or make good?

For service providers, see Chapter 4, Foundation Action Plan, under 'Manage your cash flow' (page 71) for different terms and conditions and fee options.

Intellectual property

A high percentage of any company's assets is made up of intellectual property (IP):

- brand equity – trademarks TM, registered marks ®
- processes, procedures and systems – think McDonald's
- copyright © content
- patents
- methodologies
- formulations
- software.

IP can add huge value to your company and you need to protect these assets. It could be technology or software that you've developed; a methodology you've created; content that you've developed; unique content you've created and produced on CDs, DVDs and in books. An IP lawyer will advise you how to protect different types of intellectual property.

If you have a brand that you intend growing, which is likely to produce a lot of income for your company, you will want to register it through the Trademarks Office as a registered brand. Your IP lawyer can do this for you. Once you put a fence around your intellectual property you are protecting it from others who may want to steal, use or copy it.

Legal advice and registering trademarks can be expensive, but it is important and if you start with your top priorities, ask yourself: What's most likely to be an issue? What's most important in our business?

This aspect of protection is critical. It's hard work, but please don't ignore it, because if someone goes after your IP or challenges you and tries to stop you from using it or selling it or even owning it, this is where you'll incur huge costs fighting the battle, or losing your assets. Either way you will really be putting your entire business viability at risk.

Insurances

Insurance is an important part of risk management in a growing business. Specialist advisors can sort this out for you and help you decide which type of insurance you need for your business. Here is just a short list of some types of insurance you may want to consider as part of the overall asset-protection plan for your organisation:

- **WorkCover (mandatory)** – covers costs if you or any of your employees are injured at work.
- **Professional indemnity** – protects you if a client claims your advice has had some adverse impact on them, their business, life or health.
- **Public liability** – covers you for any expenses that might result from people claiming against you, for example if somebody slips on the newly-polished floor and breaks their leg.

- **Key person** – insures against losing a key person, usually in an executive position, providing enough to cover the costs of bringing in an interim to take on the role and recruit a replacement, as well as potential loss of business until a new person has replaced the key person.

Again, I'm no expert in legal, tax or insurance matters and I recommend you find a specialist who can guide you through your protection strategies and options. They are an important part of building the structure of protection into your organisation as you grow.

Chapter worksheets

- How to implement a bonus system in your business – www.jennystilwell.com.au/sbceo/bonussystem
- Right person right role matrix – www.jennystilwell.com.au/sbceo/personrolematrix
- Blank Position Description template – www.jennystilwell.com.au/sbceo/positiondescription

Find these worksheets and tools when you go to the Small Business CEO page on the website: www.jennystilwell.com.au/sbceo

Chapter highlights

- You can't build the right structure in a growing business until you step up as the leader.
- You need to be objective about the people you have in your team and the roles you need filled.
- You need to learn how to recruit, develop and manage a team.
- People, processes and protection are key elements of Stage 2.

CHAPTER 7

Stage 3 – Business Expansion

WHEN presented with opportunities for business expansion, most business owners struggle with having confidence and certainty around which option to choose.

The key to this stage of growth is to know how to approach the process of strategy, because it can be easy to follow any or all of the opportunities in front of you, and not choose the best ones.

Do you expand geographically, or expand your product or service range, or acquire a competitor, or sell part of your business, or replicate your business model in another niche, or expand your business model? These are the sorts of questions you can face when ready for expansion.

There is no certainty of your outcomes, even with all the planning in the world. However, if you do the research into your options for business growth, and have a way to assess them strategically, you will be able to make a decision on which path to take with far more confidence and possibility of success.

Who is in Business Expansion?

- Well-established businesses that have put the necessary structure in place so they can confidently expand.
- Organisations that may have had incremental or constant results for some time, and are now looking to grow significantly – often with a view to ramp up and sell at some point in the near future.

Challenges of Business Expansion stage

- Strategic business growth – taking your company through the planning process.
- Assessing business expansion opportunities – knowing how to make the best decisions for your organisation's growth.

Taking your business through the strategic planning process

If you have several partners in your business, or a board of directors, developing a strategic plan can *sometimes* be difficult. Not all stakeholders may have an understanding of your industry, and sometimes they try to bypass any due planning process in order to impose their will to force a direction for the organisation. If this happens, a structured planning process is even more important and a fundamental key to success at this stage.

This stage of growth often happens in an ad hoc way for a lot of organisations, and decisions are based more on gut feel than a strategic process. However, businesses are likely to be more successful if they adopt a more systematic and regular approach to strategic planning and progress reviews.

Business expansion can be organic or through acquisition, or both. However, while organic growth is usually perceived as giving the CEO more control over risk, it will be slower and more incremental than growth through acquisition. Well-researched, well-planned and well-executed acquisition need not present risk that is any more severe than when a business suddenly loses a major client.

Assessing business expansion opportunities

Sometimes we pursue opportunities to grow our businesses because we want to, even though they may not be the right strategy at the time. Frequently business owners pursue expansion opportunities that are perfectly viable, but just not for now, or just not for that particular organisation.

No planning process is fail-safe and risk-free, but it makes good business sense to minimise your risk as far as possible.

Without a proper framework for decision-making, decisions can be at worst the wrong ones that use up funds and resources unnecessarily until the company gets back on track. At best, decisions made on gut feel can be the right ones, but only the owner of the business can make that decision and team commitment doesn't always follow if they haven't been involved in the process.

Keys to success in Stage 3

- By far the best way to make the best strategic decisions is to create a decision-making framework unique to your organisation, which falls naturally out of the planning process itself and is easy to develop once all the other strategic planning work has been done.
- At this stage of growth, if you have a *vision* for your organisation it will help guide your expansion decisions. Plenty of people talk about the importance of vision but they've never created one for their own business, and many

have no idea how to go about doing this. It isn't an easy exercise but at this stage of growth, you *must* have a vision with a certain degree of clarity.

- Look outside your organisation as well as inside. Understand the market in which you operate and what is coming up in terms of new business models, shifts in the customer landscape, changes to the competitor landscape, and your potential responses to those shifts. Businesses that have been well established for 20-plus years can be brought to their knees because they fail to see what is really happening in the market.

Sometimes your major client(s) will sell their business to someone who won't continue to do business with you, or for some reason you haven't entertained, they are stolen by a competitor you may have discounted. Competitors merge and acquire to become more powerful. It happens because risks are everywhere but less disruptive when you undertake a proper planning process that won't allow you to discount anything.

Don't let this happen to you.

Business Expansion examples

SUSAN – RESEARCH ORGANISATION

Susan's business had been well established for many years and had a sizeable team and client base, but had survived and grown in spite of itself. The client base was focused on a specific sector of the market, within which there were several directions the business could pursue and specialise in. New opportunities in the market were also presenting, and Susan was at a loss as to where to focus the organisation. Which direction should they take? How would she know it was the right decision? She couldn't move beyond this point because she didn't know how.

The business had grown slowly and incrementally over many years, by default rather than by design. They were sustainable and making a small profit, but could have been making far more with higher-margin projects.

Stage 3 – Business Expansion

It was time to take a strategic view for the future direction of the business.

As with many organisations in this stage, the problem was not necessarily lack of opportunity, but lack of the necessary tools that would enable them to make sound strategic decisions about their future growth.

The team and the managing director were reluctant to continue pursuing business from within their niche sector as they didn't believe it was profitable and handling the workload was too stressful for the staff. They wanted to veer away from this sector and into new directions.

> I have seen companies completely blind-sided when they lose one of their major clients because they didn't consider the possibility that this could happen.

However, several things became evident after delving deep into what was really going on in the business and with the team:

- The niche sector, which they were trying to veer away from because it was too stressful to take on projects, was in fact their ideal sector as they had considerable intellectual property to add value to clients in this space that other organisations didn't have.
- This unique IP meant they were able to charge a premium for their services, and substantially increase their operating margins and profit.
- After dissecting their proposal process we discovered that they were considerably underestimating what resources were *really* required to conduct research projects, resulting in them underquoting with very slim margins.

Once the real opportunities had been identified and screened against other options, and underlying problems had been identified, the company was able to address its strategic focus on the niche sector and set about reinforcing their premium positioning in this space.

SAM – INDUSTRIAL PRODUCTS

Sam had been in business close to 20 years and continued to grow incrementally in most years. He considered a merger as a faster way of growing – in itself, a sound strategy. However, the framework for assessing such a strategy was again absent.

Sam's ultimate strategy was a smart one. He wanted his company to have increased revenue and profit and a larger market reach to make his business a more attractive proposition for acquisition by a global company he had in mind. He saw the stepping stone was to merge with another industrial products company.

Initially, he neglected to consider what was the customer base of the company he wanted to merge with. The customer base was primarily the exact customers that he didn't want – too small and too numerous to manage effectively. On top of this, the owner of the other business wanted to stay on board for an indefinite period of time. There was actually a limited opportunity to increase profit margins. The new business would have had too many costs to carry with the same number of staff (neither MD wanted to let anyone go, which included several duplicated management roles), the retention of the two highest paid people (both the MDs), the bolting-on of a low-margin client base, and the cost of relocating two facilities on opposite sides of the city into one.

Fortunately for all concerned, this merger didn't go ahead because it was properly assessed with strategic criteria and found to be not viable.

ELKE – INTERIOR DESIGN

This organisation is a textbook case of how to build a business carefully, diligently and successfully. Elke started her business from scratch, and grew carefully to a small team. When the organisation was still only small she focused on building the brand, training the team in new products and skills, and in taking a strategic approach to growth. Elke worked long hours and ploughed any available funds back into the business.

Very early on, Elke and the team started their annual strategic planning process to set the roadmap for the year ahead. They also reviewed progress on a regular basis. Elke got a mentor and joined a mastermind group to learn the skills she was going to need as her business grew, and to focus on the future and how to get to where she wanted.

Of course business doesn't always go according to plan but this organisation's planning process keeps it focused on the right priorities at the right time. It has strategically grown its product and service portfolio, focused on the right target clients, established the right fee structures for the positioning of its business and capabilities, grown its brand, and implemented ongoing sales and marketing campaigns to grow the business.

Elke couldn't always move as quickly as she wanted to and had to fund growth from profits rather than business loans or from investors. But Elke has always worked on the strategies for growing and managing her business, and learning the skills she needed to lead her team as a cohesive unit.

The early years were extremely hard work and demanding, but now all her strategic work is paying off. Elke has built considerable value into her business – a future acquirer will pay a premium for that value when the time is right.

Top 3 strategies to use in Stage 3

- Prepare yourself and your team for the strategic planning process, and do the analysis work required to fully understand your business situation and what you may need in order to expand.
- Develop a decision-making framework so you can confidently assess expansion opportunities and select the best ones for your business at the time.
- Create a strategic roadmap that your team can easily refer to in order to stay on track, with clear action plans for each strategy. Execution is key.

This stage could continue for many years and this is how global companies become so large – a continuous cycle of expansion, mostly through acquisition, and consolidating structure.

Chapter highlights

- Businesses can falter at Stage 3 if they fail to consider their options strategically.
- The only way to make sure you are choosing the best growth options for your business is to have a strategic framework in place to help you assess your opportunities for expansion.
- If you haven't analysed the important aspects of your business, your strategy process will be flawed and you could make poor decisions.

CHAPTER 8

Stage 3 Action Plan – Business Expansion

BUSINESS expansion needs a strategic focus. Clients I have worked with say they want to take their organisation to the next stage. However, they have not fully considered what it will take to make that happen, or what the consequences of that growth will be. Others are driven to grow, build and ultimately sell for the big payday. They typically become more strategic as they get closer to the vision for selling, taking time out to plan and consider their options.

What doesn't change for anyone in the Business Expansion stage is the need for a strategic approach to growth. You have far more at risk if you make decisions based on gut feel than you did when your business was a start-up.

I know that having a process that you can work through – a clear framework for strategic decision-making, not just based on gut feel – is a relief. It takes the guesswork out of setting direction for your organisation, and makes your strategic priorities instantly clear.

As the CEO of a public company, you can't make decisions based on gut feel when you are answerable to a board and shareholders. As CEO of your own unlisted organisation, you may not be answerable to anyone but yourself, and maybe your family, but why take the risk and leave strategy up to gut feel?

I know that once you start driving your business using the strategic approach explained here, you will continue to use it year in and year out because it will give you clarity, confidence, certainty and control.

Here is a recap of the top three strategies for Stage 3, Business Expansion:

- Do the work of analysis to identify what's really going on in your business.
- Develop a decision-making framework to guide you.
- Create a strategic roadmap for you and your team to execute.

Getting strategic is a big topic, so there are multiple parts to these priorities. In order to keep this as manageable as possible, the next section is in worksheet format as much as possible so you can actually see examples and how to do this analysis.

We won't go into every area of your business, but we will focus more in-depth analysis on the key areas where you make money – products and services, your clients, and your people who produce and support this moneymaking activity.

There are three tools included here for you:

- The Strategic Planning Preplist™
- The Strategic Mini-Review
- The Strategic SWOT.

These are all essential components of your background strategy work – they apply to all businesses.

If I were leading your organisation through a strategic retreat, I would customise this analytical approach for your business. For this book, the generic approach is all you need to start with.

Strategic Planning Preplist™

This is a warm-up thinking exercise to start pulling together the information you need to base your strategic planning on. You cannot create a strategic plan without collecting information – including feedback from your team and your customers – analysing your business, and addressing all the key components that form part of the plan.

The purpose of the Strategic Planning Preplist™ is to:

- get you thinking more strategically about the growth of your business
- identify areas where you need to focus for change and improvement, to capitalise on opportunity, or even to investigate and analyse further
- give you a foundation before you move onto the next step of the planning process – the in-depth strategic review
- provide a tool for your team to engage in the process of answering these questions and giving feedback at this early stage.

As you go through this list of questions; I want you to think long and hard about your answers. Make notes, write down the answers, and add any other questions that come to mind. If any question raises alarm bells or compels you to dive deeper into an area, chances are it needs closer attention.

There are three parts. The first asks big-picture questions about you and your relationship with the business; the second asks more specific questions about different functional areas in the business; the third covers bigger-picture questions. All are equally important and I recommend you spend as much time as you need to answer the questions to the best of your knowledge.

Part 1: You and your impact on the business

1. Do you feel fulfilled?

- Are you happy with the contribution you are making?
- Are you happy with the value you are creating for your clients, yourself and others?
- Are you happy with your progress to date?
- Do you look forward to each day, or are you bored?
- Do you want more of the same or something different?
- If you were to start your business all over again, is this where you'd want to be?

2. Are you still learning and growing?

If not, it's almost impossible to grow your business.

- Are you reading, learning, thinking and forming new ideas continually?
- When was the last time you had a conversation that sparked new thinking and new ideas for your business?
- What is on your reading list?
- Where do you get new ideas from?

3. Are your standards high enough?

- How influential are you?
- How influential is/are your business/products/services?
- Are you performing at your best? If not, what is holding you back?
- Could your standards for yourself and your business be higher?

- What could be possible for your business, and your life, if you stepped up and held yourself accountable to higher standards?

4. Do your beliefs align with the goals you have for your business?

If there is a gap between the goals you *want* for your business and the goals you *believe* you can achieve, you will fall short of achieving your goal every time. Your belief system will keep you in the realm of what you *know* you are able to achieve. It's only when you truly believe you can achieve much more, that you will start to do so.

- Are your goals limited by what you believe is possible?
- What do you really believe about how far you could take your business?
- Do you need to stretch your thinking to form a new perspective of what's possible, and believe it?

5. How could innovation change your outcomes?

- Honestly, is your business like all the others in your industry or is it different?
- Who is creating the best innovation in your industry, globally?
- Which companies in other industries are doing innovative things that you could adapt for your organisation?
- Do you do anything at all that is innovative? If not, what could be your first initiative?

Part 2: Functional areas of the business

1. Clients and referrers

- Do we really know our target market? Can we describe the profile of our ideal clients?

- Are we close enough to our clients that we know what (else) they really want that we could deliver to them?
- Do we acknowledge and nurture our best customers and referrers?

2. Product/service portfolio

When assessing products, think about factors like length of sales cycle, volume of sales, margin, repeat sales, etc.

- Which product or service lines are most profitable and make the greatest margin contribution to the business?
- Do we need to change the mix of our product/service portfolio in any way?
- Are our products and services easy to sell, easy to buy and easy to use/work with (the last two criteria being from the client perspective)? These three questions alone can be insightful.
- When did we last review our fees and pricing?

3. Key measurements

Consider, for example, revenue per employee versus profit per employee; sales per product/service versus margin contribution per product/service.

- Do we know what the key measurements are to assess the overall progress and performance of the business, and can we report on that?
- Are we tracking and comparing performance on previous years to identify trends and drivers of growth?

4. CEO thinking and decisions

- What will drive our business growth strategy this year? Will growth be from our core business and customers, or from somewhere new?

Stage 3 Action Plan – Business Expansion

- Where did our business growth come from last year, and was it enough?
- Will we need funding for our growth strategy? What options do we have?
- Where is the biggest exposure/risk in the business? What needs to be done to address it?
- What changes could I make, as the CEO, in what I do to improve the performance of the business?
- Is the whole organisation clear on our competitive advantage (organisation-focused) and our value proposition (customer-focused)?
- Can we all actually see where we are going with the business, and could we describe what that looks like in three years' time?

5. **Infrastructure – people, processes, protection**

- Do we have processes and systems in place for the most important parts of our business?
- Do we have the right team of A- and B-people with no Cs? Do we have resource gaps?
- Do we have the right commercial structure in place for our business – legal and financial?
- Where is the inherent value in our business? Have we protected our intellectual property?
- Have we protected key relationships with partners with service agreements? Are they sustainable?
- Have we fully considered service and support resourcing and costs as we grow?

6. **Sales and marketing**

- Are we aiming at the top-end, mid-tier or mass market? Why is this our strategy?

- Are sales tracking against the targets we set, by client?
- Are we measuring our marketing activities? Are they giving us the return on investment we expected?
- Could we be doing anything more or better in sales and marketing to grow the business?

Part 3: Bigger-picture considerations

You can gather information from your financials, sales reports, customer feedback, employee feedback in order to answer these questions. Answer the tough questions you pose yourself as honestly as you possibly can.

1. Organic growth versus acquisition

Speed, funding and execution are essential elements required with an acquisition. Organic growth is more manageable but slower. Acquisition can speed things up considerably but is an undertaking that hijacks the attention of those tasked with project-managing it, away from the day-to-day operations of the organisation and towards assessing, planning and executing the acquisition.

- Have you factored into your analysis the costs associated with acquisitions – legal, financial, specialist advisors, possible retrenchments or relocation to another facility?
- Are there more costs you should consider?
- Is acquisition the best strategy for your business right now?
- Will the synergies of the acquisition produce a real return on investment for you?
- Can you achieve your growth goals with organic growth fast enough?

2. Leverage

Always consider the leverage you can gain for your business from technology, existing assets and relationships.

- Do you have underutilised real estate you could lease out?
- Could you scale up faster and ramp up your customer base with technology?
- Do you have opportunities to partner with key relationships for business expansion?
- Is there leverage within your own database to expand and grow?

The strategic mini-review

In order to develop the right strategies for where your business is at, you need to be able to see it through a more strategic lens. This mini-review gives you three simple strategies to apply to your business right now. They will help to align your focus onto the right strategies for the best outcomes in three key areas – your customers, your products and services, and your people.

Remember: in order to make decisions in your business regarding customers, products or services and number of people you employ, you will need to delve deeper into all the circumstances and considerations within your own organisation.

These strategies are first steps to help you start taking control of your business today. So, let's move onto the first strategy!

Assess the value of your customers

Assessing and understanding what's really going on in your customer base – and getting the mix right – can transform your business. More customers need more servicing, more management and usually more people. Some will be a good fit for your business and others won't. Some will be profitable and others won't.

Here's a strategic tool for how to drill down a level into your customer base.

Action plan

1. Do the client value spreadsheet

Enter all your customers from the last three years (or five if you have that information available) into a spreadsheet. Include the following fields in this order from the left=hand column across to the right:

a. Company/client name

b. Total annual value 3 years ago

c. Total annual value 2 years ago

d. Total annual value last year

e. Total cumulative value.

Note: If you don't have this information easily available, ask your accountant, bookkeeper or finance manager to do this exercise for you.

Your client value spreadsheet for the last three years will look something like Table 8.1 below, depending on how many clients or customers you have.

As you can see, Acme Trading and Diablo Actuaries have been inactive over the last couple of years, and may need reactivating. If they can't be reactivated, they may not be the right customers for this business. Tuck Fabrics and Slapdash Cleaning are only new in the last year and may grow to be larger, more valuable customers in the next few years.

Stage 3 Action Plan – Business Expansion

Table 8.1: Client value assessment – for Amiable Accountants Inc. (Alphabetical)

Client name	Value 2014 ($)	Value 2015 ($)	Value 2016 ($)	Total value ($)
ABC Software	–	3,200	2,700	5,900
About Face Cosmetics	2,800	2,600	5,500	10,900
Acme Trading	1,200	1,800	–	3,000
Altmodisch Architects	15,000	23,500	17,900	56,400
Beesting Beauty	1,000	1,900	1,800	4,700
Butch Building Company	34,700	22,900	11,800	69,400
Cinderella Interiors	–	7,600	–	7,600
Diablo Actuaries	6,700	–	–	6,700
Eaglehawk Ventures	9,800	21,000	28,700	59,500
Horatio Ceramics	2,400	3,900	8,760	15,060
Kitsch Kitchens	29,200	8,500	6,600	44,300
Machiavelli Marketing	–	3,400	2,100	5,500
Nouvelle Catering	2,700	3,000	7,800	13,500
Poseidon Pools	21,200	26,800	33,000	81,000
Roughshod Landscapers	4,600	6,400	12,000	23,000
Slapdash Cleaning	–	–	3,200	3,200
Tuck Fabrics	–	–	4,600	4,600
Winston Watches	6,700	790	560	8,050
Total ($)	**138,000**	**137,290**	**147,020**	**422,310**

2. Sort by total value column

There are many other considerations when doing this analysis, but let's keep it simple and look at the total combined value of the client over the last three years. That includes the total amount they've spent with you each year on your entire product/service range.

What stands out here is that four customers have generated far more revenue for this organisation than the others.

3. Divide your customer values into four or five tiers

These tiers are arbitrary tiers set by you, so define them into logical groupings.

In our example, the logical tiers have been defined as:

- Tier 1: $50,000–100,000
- Tier 2: $20,000–50,000
- Tier 3: $10,000–20,000
- Tier 4: <$10,000.

The purpose of this exercise is to identify a number of factors:

- Is the overall value of your clients increasing, constant or declining?
- What is the growth trend for individual clients?
- What is the value of your customer tiers – where do you want to focus?
- Do you want to divest any of your clients?
- Are there opportunities to grow any clients into a higher tier?
- Are any of your clients inactive and need to be reactivated?
- What are your best clients worth to your business?
- What differentiates your best clients from the others, i.e. what do they need that makes them higher value?

Stage 3 Action Plan – Business Expansion

Table 8.2: Client value assessment – for Amiable Accountants Inc. (Sorted by total value)

Client name	Value 2014 ($)	Value 2015 ($)	Value 2016 ($)	Total value ($)
Poseidon Pools	21,200	26,800	33,000	81,000
Butch Building Company	34,700	22,900	11,800	69,400
Eaglehawk Ventures	9,800	21,000	28,700	59,500
Altmodisch Architects	15,000	23,500	17,900	56,400
Kitsch Kitchens	29,200	8,500	6,600	44,300
Roughshod Landscapers	4,600	6,400	12,000	23,000
Horatio Ceramics	2,400	3,900	8,760	15,060
Nouvelle Catering	2,700	3,000	7,800	13,500
About Face Cosmetics	2,800	2,600	5,500	10,900
Winston Watches	6,700	790	560	8,050
Cinderella Interiors	–	7,600	–	7,600
Diablo Actuaries	6,700	–	–	6,700
ABC Software	–	3,200	2,700	5,900
Machiavelli Marketing	–	3,400	2,100	5,500
Beesting Beauty	1,000	1,900	1,800	4,700
Tuck Fabrics	–	–	4,600	4,600
Slapdash Cleaning	–	–	3,200	3,200
Acme Trading	1,200	1,800	–	3,000
Total ($)	**138,000**	**137,290**	**147,020**	**422,310**

As you can see from Table 8.3 overleaf, 79% of sales revenue comes from 33% of the customer base – six clients in Tiers 1 and 2. The other 21% of sales comes from the other two-thirds of the customer base.

If Amiable Accountants were to acquire another six clients the same as those in Tiers 1 and 2, it would make a significant difference to its revenue.

Table 8.3: Breakdown of customers by value tiers for Amiable Accountants Inc.

Customer value tier	No. of customers/tier	Sales revenue ($)	% of total sales (%)
1. $50,000+	4	266,300	63
2. $20 to 50,000	2	67,300	16
3. $10 to 20,000	3	39,460	9
4. <$10,000	9	49,250	12
	18	422,310	

With this information, you can set sales targets for the next year, you can allocate account managers based on the value of the customers, and you can focus your resources on where the majority of your sales come from.

Client value tiers – a worksheet for your business

Follow the above example and fill in the worksheet (Table 8.4) for your own business. At this point, you can add another column and add in the forecast revenue for the current year for each of your clients. This will enable you to see how each client is tracking in their 'value tier' and if their spend with you is growing, constant or declining. If you aren't comfortable including the forecast sales figures for the current year, just do this analysis based on actual sales for preceding years.

Stage 3 Action Plan – Business Expansion

Table 8.4: Client value worksheet

Client name	Value 3 years ago ($)	Value 2 years ago ($)	Value last year ($)	Total value ($)
Total ($)				

4. Summarise what you've identified

_____ % of my customer base generates _____ % of revenue

I can break my customers up into _____ tiers.

The tiers have the following values:

Tier 1 _____

Tier 2 _____

Tier 3 _____

etc.

My ideal customers are like those in Tiers _____ and _____.

The customers who add little overall value to the revenue and profit of the company are in Tiers _____ and _____.

To get better results we need to focus on our ideal customers' worth around $_____ per year in sales revenue.

Note: Many customers may start small, in a low tier, and grow to become your best and most valuable customers. You will need to evaluate each customer in terms of their current tier and the tier they could grow into.

If you take your eye off this analysis and aren't close enough to all your most valuable customers, you may miss the fact that you are about to lose one. This happens for many reasons: they get acquired, they sell, they no longer need your services as the project/original need has been fulfilled or they are lured away by a competitor who gives them more attention than you do.

Assess the value of your products and services

You may have multiple streams of revenue from different products, services, or different brands. You may develop them in-house, or sell someone else's products. Either way, it's not just

Stage 3 Action Plan – Business Expansion

about the sales revenue. What's also important is the contribution these products make to your margin. Some products deliver more to your business with less effort, while others consume resources and add complexity to your business.

In order to put product complexity into perspective, think of a range of hair care products. One range may have five different types of hair styling product. Each type comes in two different sizes. The range therefore has ten stock keeping units (SKUs).

Compare this to a range that has seven different types of shampoo and matching conditioner. Each comes in two different sizes, and each comes in a travel size pack as well. This range would have 42 SKUs.

The more SKUs you have in your product range, the more inventory you need to manage. You need to sell in these ranges to your distribution channel, manage stock orders and replenishment, manage the cost of mark downs, slow moving and obsolete stock and warehouse them in your own facility or through a third party.

All these SKUs and associated costs need to be factored in when you assess the profitability of your product and individual ranges. An example is given in Table 8.5 to highlight this:

Table 8.5: Margin contribution analysis by product

	Product 1	Product 2	Product 3	Product 4	Total
Sales revenue ($)	5,675,000	2,100,000	4,750,000	1,135,000	13,660,000
COGS ($)	2,270,000	924,000	2,137,500	703,700	6,035,200
Margin ($)	3,405,000	1,176,000	2,612,500	431,300	7,624,800
Margin (%)	60	56	55	**38**	
% of total margin	45	15	34	**6**	
% of total sales	42	15	35	**8**	100

Note:

1. Product 1 is clearly the superstar, contributing $3.4 million and 45% of the total operating margin, and 42% of total sales.
2. Products 2 and 3 are strong performers with healthy margins and sales results.
3. On the other hand, the danger is in Product 4 – it contributes only 8% to sales and 6% to the organisation's overall margin.
4. This scenario can occur, for example, where the good performers are the organisation's own products, and the lower-margin products are third-party products.
5. Decisions about which products to keep and which to divest need to be made in the larger context of all considerations.

Stage 3 Action Plan – Business Expansion

Table 8.6: Margin contribution analysis by product complexity (no. of SKUs)

	Product 1	Product 2	Product 3	Product 4	Total
Sales revenue ($)	5,675,000	2,100,000	4,750,000	1,135,000	13,660,000
COGS ($)	2,270,000	924,000	2,137,500	703,700	6,035,200
Margin ($)	3,405,000	1,176,000	2,612,500	431,300	7,624,800
Margin (%)	60	56	55	38	
% of total margin	45	15	34	6	
% of total sales	42	15	35	8	100
SKUs	13	41	35	**88**	177
% of total SKUs	7	23	20	**50**	100

Note:

1. If these products are all tangible and have stock keeping units (SKUs), another factor to consider is how many SKUs exist for each product line. This inventory needs to be stored, picked and packed, replenished, kept track of and reported on. This costs money, requires people and systems and infrastructure, and can add considerable complexity to your business if not managed well.

2. If we add SKUs to this example we can further see that our star product is a tight product range with only 13 SKUs, whereas our 'danger' product not only has low margins but carries 50% of the organisation's total SKUs.

Action plan

1. Find this information for your own product/service range.

If you don't have access to this information, ask your accountant to provide a contribution analysis for all your products.

2. Fill in Table 8.7 for your own product/service range.

The following matrix is blank for you to fill in.

Table 8.7: Margin contribution by product matrix

	Product 1	Product 2	Product 3	Product 4	Total
Sales revenue ($)					
COGS ($)					
Margin ($)					
Margin (%)					
% of total margin					
% of total sales					
SKUs					
% of total SKUs (%)					

Stage 3 Action Plan – Business Expansion

3. *Summarise your results*

The star products that contribute the most to our operating margin are

_____

_____

Products that require the most management and overheads are

_____

_____

If we factor in the real cost of managing our different products (people, warehouse, reporting, compliance etc.), the low performers are

_____

_____

The strong/reliable performers are

_____

_____

The products we need to focus more on are

_____

_____

The products we will analyse further to identify whether we gradually divest /reduce/replace are

_____

_____

Assess the contribution of your people

This exercise is designed to show you the return you are making on your team *as a whole*. You expect a return on investment from all the assets and resources employed by your company. You need a return on investment from your people. If you have too many employees relative to your organisation's turnover, your costs are going to be higher than they need to be.

The goal is a balancing act between minimising costs, operating as efficiently as you can – good people, good systems and processes, good reporting on key performance indicators – and having the right number of people employed for the current level of business you're doing.

Revenue per employee and profit per employee are good indicators:

- They tell you how many people you are using to get the results you are getting.
- Your headcount will rise to both drive and support your sales revenue, but it needs to be relative.
- If your indicators are declining year-on-year as your turnover grows, e.g. lower sales per employee, it means you're being less efficient in your use of resources. It often means you haven't streamlined your procedures and put better systems in place to support growth.
- Business owners often throw people at problems rather than first solving the problems and making the business run more efficiently. This combination of not having good systems and adding more people to help manage your business increases complexity and costs.

Stage 3 Action Plan – Business Expansion

Action plan

1. You've already got your sales figures from the first exercise, so refer to those total sales revenue figures for the last three to five years.
2. Also note down the total people employed (full-time equivalent) for each of the corresponding years.

Table 8.8: Example 1: Revenue and profit per employee

	Revenue 3 years ago ($)	Revenue 2 years ago	Revenue last year	Forecast revenue this year ($)
	6,100,000	7,500,000	10,000,000	12,000,000
No. of employees	16	19	17	17
Revenue per employee ($)	381,250	395,000	588,000	706,000
Net profit ($)	550,000	600,000	1,000,000	2,000,000
Net profit per employee ($)	34,375	31,578	58,823	117,647

Notes:

1. Table 8.8 shows that revenue per employee is climbing. Sales have virtually doubled with approximately the same number of people over the three to four years.
2. Profit has grown considerably overall and per employee, which would indicate that the organisation is doing things far more efficiently with the same number of people.
3. It could also indicate that the current team are being pushed to their limits and more people now need to be brought onboard. To evaluate that, you need to talk to your team, get

their feedback and assess their performance and stress levels, and also assess how smoothly your operations are working.

Summarise your findings

Our average revenue per employee has been (circle which one):

- constant
- increasing
- decreasing.

Average profit per employee has been:

- constant
- increasing
- decreasing.

I know the causes behind the trends in our indicators – yes / no.

Our business is no more / somewhat / a lot more complex than it was a few years ago.

Our overall operations run smoothly / somewhat smoothly / with more and more glitches.

We may need to increase / reduce the number of employees

We may need to improve our systems and efficiencies – yes / no.

Next steps

Based on the findings from your three strategies, what actions could you implement now to reduce the complexity in your business, improve the overall performance, or take the summary points from this strategic mini-review to the next stage? Note these findings in the space provided below.

Stage 3 Action Plan – Business Expansion

1. _____

2. _____

3. _____

4. _____

5. _____

6. _____

This review should shed some light on what may be driving the complexity in your business, what needs to change and how your focus may need to shift. By using these three mini-strategies to delve into what's really going on in your business, you will have an indicator of some of the priorities you may decide to address. If you're feeling overwhelmed, then focus on one strategy at a time.

With the 'next steps' I recommend you set some timeframes around the actions and schedule them into your diary. Get help if you need to.

For the complete workbook on how to systematically analyse and grow your client base, including appropriate account management strategies, go to www.jennystilwell.com.au/sbceo-guide

The strategic SWOT analysis

Often people conduct a SWOT analysis for their business, fill in the points under each heading, and then don't do any more with it – few people seem to know how to use it strategically in their planning. Figure 8.1 is an example of a simple strategic SWOT analysis. But before we start filling it out, here's the low-down:

Figure 8.1: SWOT analysis template

Internal	**Strengths**	**Weaknesses**
External	**Opportunities**	**Threats**

What is a SWOT analysis?

A SWOT analysis is a strategic tool used in planning, such as marketing plans and business plans. You could do a SWOT on yourself, a product, a project, a business unit, as well as on your overall business. It's an objective look at the internal and external factors affecting your business, summarised into strengths, weaknesses, opportunities and threats.

Strengths and weaknesses are internal factors that reside or exist within your business. Opportunities and threats exist outside and separate from your business, but can impact your business.

The purpose of conducting a SWOT analysis is to enable you to perform more competitively within the environment in which you operate or plan to operate. When you do an objective SWOT,

Stage 3 Action Plan – Business Expansion

you'll be able to match your resources more efficiently and effectively to your environment, for greater success.

How does it work?

The person who develops the strategic plan for your business could also do the SWOT analysis. Your whole team could be involved in the process so you have their perspectives as well, or it could be developed by a few who have a more comprehensive perspective of the overall business.

> When you do an objective SWOT, you'll be able to match your resources more efficiently and effectively to your environment, for greater success.

A useful approach is to combine SWOT feedback and then review it during a workshop-type session. You will cover off a lot of information about internal and external environments, encourage discussion about the real strengths, weaknesses, opportunities and threats, and lay a solid foundation for the strategic planning process.

Here are some typical examples that could fall under each of the categories:

Strengths
- capable team – make sure it's in all areas of the business, because if it isn't, then you have a weakness somewhere – e.g. product development and sales are strong, but customer service is weak
- intellectual property – trademarks, patents; brand recognition based on research rather than opinion
- client base
- marketing system
- office facilities
- low cost base

- technology
- production capacity – available for growth.

Often during this exercise I receive responses like 'everyone gets on well'. This is a good thing, but not necessarily a strength. As a litmus test, ask yourself: Does having this make us more competitive/more profitable and more attractive to our target market?

Weaknesses
- lack of specialist resources
- limited IP
- incomplete and out-of-date customer database
- small distribution network
- low profile within target market
- poor accounting system, i.e. can't accurately measure and track KPIs
- production capacity unused – wasted resources and costs.

Opportunities
- alliance with a potential business partner e.g. expand distribution network
- new technology to reduce costs, improve processes
- new market expansion – increase sales
- emerging customer needs e.g. new products/services and sales.

Threats
- entry of strong competitors to this market from other markets
- new technology renders your products/services redundant
- new legislation restricts business.

How do I use it?

Now that you've done the SWOT, you need to apply what it's uncovered to your strategy. Partner your SWOT factors as shown in Table 8.9 below:

Table 8.9: An example SWOT analysis

	Strengths	Weaknesses
Opportunities	Strength/Opportunity strategies Capitalise	Weakness/Opportunity strategies Overcome and capitalise
Threats	Strength/Threat strategies Minimise	Weakness/Threat strategies Defend

Strengths and Opportunities (S–O) strategies

Use your inherent strengths to capitalise on available opportunities that fit with your overall business purpose and goals. For example, you may have a large customer base as a strength, and also have the opportunity to take on new technology that would enable you to deliver superior service to your clients/deliver more/deliver faster/deliver more cheaply – all of which could increase sales, improve margins, and ultimately increase your profitability.

Weaknesses and Threats (W–T) strategies

Develop a strategy to protect the business from the weaknesses that make it highly vulnerable to the most likely threats. For example, if a weakness is limited IP (intellectual property) and a threat is entry into your market by strong competitors, then your defensive strategy could be to develop or acquire IP that makes you more competitive and gives you a point of difference in the market.

Strengths and Threats (S–T) strategies

Use your strengths to minimise the most likely threats to your business. For example, if a solid distribution network is a strength, you may decide to channel more products into that distribution network to gain more market share, minimising the potential market share for any new competitor.

Weaknesses and Opportunities (W–O) strategies

Develop a strategy to overcome or remove the weaknesses in your business in order to take advantage of the opportunities that exist for growth/increased profit/market share, etc. For example, if you have a lack of specialist resources but have an opportunity to partner with another organisation to take on their products/services, you could make it a priority to bring specialist resources into your business to enable you to quickly take advantage of that opportunity. You want to be ready to:

- take advantage of the best opportunities for your business
- ward off any threats that could significantly impact your business.

You don't want to adopt strategies that:

- further highlight a weakness in your business
- add more pressure to already strained resources
- place you in a market where you are unable to compete effectively.

A SWOT analysis is a sorting tool – it helps you sort the best strategies from a list of options, and provides a framework to identify your most important priorities. These priority strategies go into your decision-making framework to be assessed against other opportunities. Pick your top three to five most important strategies.

If you only do part of this exercise without working through all the combinations, you're leaving yourself open to risk and/or lost opportunities.

Develop a decision-making framework

Now that you've worked through all the analysis of your business, you will have identified the following:

- priority areas that you need to address
- a list of strategies to address your weaknesses and shore up against your threats
- a list of opportunities available to expand your business.

Working through the Strategic SWOT has now made you aware, if you weren't before, of the threats and weaknesses that will form part of your decision-making framework. You need to be aware of these threats and weaknesses – they are some of the criteria you will be assessing your opportunities against.

You also have a full list of all the opportunities that your business has right now. It is these opportunities that you will make decisions about once the decision-making framework is in place.

Strategic considerations for the framework

You can incorporate all, or just a few, of these criteria into your framework, as well as use others not listed here. Select what is appropriate for your business.

ROI

Overall, ROI (return on investment) is what you are trying to determine. If you pursue a specific opportunity, is it likely to yield a worthwhile return on investment of your time and resources?

You can keep it simple for this summary exercise and use a scale of L (low), M (medium) or H (high) to indicate different levels of potential value/ROI. Your ROI may be negligible in Year 1 but high by Year 3, for example, or high in the first few months. Again, it depends on the opportunity, the model, the market and other factors.

I like to use 'potential value in plan period' as a criterion, because if the opportunity will take time to develop beyond your current planning period, it is a longer-term opportunity that will probably require further review and analysis.

Once you have made the decision that an opportunity is a high priority, if it doesn't check everything in your decision-making framework and requires capital investment, additional people, or even a change to your business model, you will need to do a more in-depth analysis of the opportunity. Costs, the model, projections, timeframe, assumptions and market tests – all will help indicate potential returns.

Market testing

If possible, testing your product or service or new business opportunity is always preferable. You can test prototypes, beta versions of your offer, ideas and concepts with your customers and clients.

Stage 3 Action Plan – Business Expansion

Giving away free samples to the public is a way of testing products, services and food. University campuses, music festivals and local shopping centres are all ways to capture feedback from the public and test your product at the same time.

When I was responsible for international marketing of a brand-new product in my young corporate career, we had a model: test the product, test the distribution channel, test the market.

Testing the product involved considerable market research, development of prototypes that we tested, and focus-group testing of the first products. Testing the distribution channels was to ensure we got the type of distributor right for this new type of telephony product. Had we profiled the distributors correctly and would they be able to sell our new phone systems? Finally, we tested the market with a small launch in a small market.

Always test in a small market so you contain the test. If successful, roll it out to other markets; if unsuccessful, try other small markets or withdraw and regroup with minimal damage.

Autonomy

Do you retain or lose autonomy? For some small business CEOs, losing autonomy in their business is a deal-breaker. For others, they may think they're prepared to share autonomy when they merge their business with another to create a much bigger entity, but in reality this doesn't end well – because it isn't executed well.

Assumptions

It's always smart to know what assumptions you're working from when considering each strategic opportunity. This goes hand-in-hand with considering the downside. If you're considering investing a million dollars in new plant and equipment, or custom-built technology that will change your business model, being clear about the assumptions you're making and the potential risk is essential.

Risk

There are different methodologies for assessing risk, but for this exercise keep it simple. Use a scale of 1–5 where 5 is highest risk and 1 is lowest.

In order to think about risks in a context that will be useful for this process, ask yourself: What could be the downside? People get harmed, the economy changes, there's a natural disaster, the exchange rate varies by x%, technology makes our model redundant, etc. Only you can draw out the answers to this question for your expansion plans.

Speed

How quickly will you be able to realise the opportunity being reviewed? Can it be done quickly or will it be a slow option? Again, these are all parts of the consideration when comparing different opportunities. I often use the criterion of whether it falls into the Plan Period, as in, can we capitalise on this opportunity in the next 12 months, if that's your planning period. It's a useful reference.

Funding

External funding, if required, may put one opportunity lower down the priority list than another that is self-funded. Again, that consideration needs to be weighed up against all the others. It all depends on your risk appetite and whether you would consider external funding to enable you to capitalise on a strategic opportunity, or if you would prefer to go down the self-funded path. The choice will be an individual one.

Existing people

Can the opportunity you are considering be capitalised on by your existing team or will it require investment in additional resources? If you require additional resources, make sure that you factor the costs of adding people into the overall detailed assessment of the opportunity.

Existing business model

For those of you old enough to remember, the dot.com boom was a strange time to be in the technology sector. People invested in companies they didn't really understand, in 'platforms' and 'portals' they could barely explain if asked, and in anything internet.

Imagine, for example, if a market leader in a traditional technology space with a strong B2B model were to invest in an ISP –internet service provider – whose sole purpose was to attract a mass consumer market.

That would be a big cross against each of the criteria here. And when the business model doesn't fit and you don't hive it off as a separate business with appropriate resources and core capabilities, it is unlikely to succeed.

Core competencies

Does the new opportunity you are considering match with your organisation's core competencies? A company I once worked for decided to make a complete shift away from the software it had been developing and marketing for years, primarily with corporate IT management as its customers, to become a supplier of tele-marketing systems to the banking industry. On every level, there was no match to the organisation's existing core competencies. What happened in this scenario could be the content for a whole other book, but suffice it to say that this new strategy was deeply challenged from the outset!

Potential sales value

This is difficult to assess without detailed projections. However, if you are developing or bringing in a new product that you would sell to your existing customer base or clients, it is much easier to make some estimates on likely uptake by known clients.

If your opportunity is for a brand-new market, this is harder to assess in terms of the likely sales you would make. An estimated dollar value is preferred, but if you haven't done the numbers, your initial estimate could simply be Low, Medium or High. Having said that, if you decide to pursue an opportunity because potential sales value is 'High', you really need to do the work and analyse what sort of number 'High' would actually be!

Projected revenue, infrastructure and expenses all need to be assessed for a brand-new venture.

Sales cycle

If your business is technology, you may have some entry-level software with a very short sales cycle. You may sell many multiples of these products in a day or a week. If you sell high-end systems that have a starting price of several hundred thousand dollars, and escalate as the software is customised, your sales cycle is obviously much longer and you would be more likely to sell far fewer of these systems than your other products. They take much longer to sell. This of course impacts your cash flow and you must consider it in your strategic decision-making around which opportunities to pursue as a priority.

Fulfilment factor

This may seem like an odd inclusion in a list alongside risk profile, ROI and funding. However, I think it's an essential inclusion in your decision-making process when talking about *your* business, especially if there are things other than profit and money that motivate you. You may want to build your business to a point where you are able to set up a foundation for charitable projects, or you may want to create something with a more far-reaching legacy. Whatever makes you feel good about what you are doing in and with your business, it is that thing which provides fulfilment. If this is really important to you, you must include it in the framework.

Align with vision

Hopefully you have a vision for your business! I haven't included the process to map that out in this book. For now, let's say you know where you're taking the business and what picture you are creating. The opportunities that you pursue need to align with that vision for your future. Asking the question about alignment with vision helps keep you on track, with all your opportunities in perspective.

These considerations should have been covered when you worked through the strategic SWOT and came up with your list of strategies. If you didn't get that far, you may want to include these criteria in your decision-making framework:

Capitalise on strengths

Does an opportunity capitalise on your strengths? If it doesn't, you may give it a low priority for now and evaluate at another time.

Minimise weaknesses

The objective is to minimise weaknesses rather than intensify them. Some strategies will demand that you address your weaknesses so that you are able to take advantage of a new opportunity.

Reduce threats

Not all strategies that you pursue will reduce your exposure to threats, but wherever possible it is preferable that they do, particularly if the threats are real and considerable.

Selecting your criteria

The criteria you select for your decision-making framework will be those that enable you to make a high-level decision on which opportunities you will prioritise in the next 12 months. Any requiring further research or analysis can be allocated to someone in your team or a small project team, or you may take it on yourself as a special project to work on further.

Example – packaging design company

Table 8.10 on pages 190 to 191 is an example for a packaging design company, and how it assessed and then prioritised the main opportunities available to them. This packaging design company has straightforward opportunities: growing existing client value, developing new product and service ranges, opening another office/expanding into a new geographic area, acquiring a similar business to significantly grow, starting an online sales channel, and bringing in-house some of the supply chain to control the design process, reduce costs, increase margin and increase speed of delivery to the customer.

You can see that based on the ticks – low potential risk and potential value – why the first three opportunities are the top priorities for this organisation.

This framework helps put them in perspective against each other, and in terms of timeframe and potential value. It is an extremely helpful tool in giving you clarity about your immediate priorities.

This example looks simple and it's meant to. When you use it for your own business, and for opportunities that are more complex and can involve significant investment in capital, sourcing or producing offshore, merging with a similar business, franchising, licensing or acquisitions, then it is a great screening and sorting tool for giving you the right focus at the right time.

Stage 3 Action Plan – Business Expansion

In the next section we put this all together into an action plan. Everything up to here has been to enable you to decide on which strategies and which opportunities, with certainty and clarity. Then you need to get to work on each, and get into action.

Strategic roadmap

Once you have your list of prioritised opportunities, you need to convert each one into a series of actions, including who will be responsible and when the actions need to be completed by. The person whose name is against each main action is responsible for taking care that all the subactions are completed as part of the process (see Table 8.11 on page 192).

With this roadmap everyone in your team knows exactly what they are responsible for and what the whole organisation is working towards. You can use these action sheets in your regular management meetings to track progress and hold everyone accountable.

Let's assume that the packaging design company in the previous example settled on the top three ranked opportunities to focus on, and decided to investigate further Item 7 – the acquisition of supply-chain components to reduce cost and improve turnaround on delivery.

As the top three opportunities progress throughout the year, this organisation may have quarterly, half-yearly or annual strategic reviews, at which point they can revisit the other opportunities on their original list. These may then be reassessed and either taken on as priorities or investigated further, or they may be no longer relevant.

It's always a good idea to revisit your new opportunities on an ongoing basis, and to repeat this entire exercise regularly. Dates and progress can be monitored and adjusted accordingly on a

Table 8.10: Example decision-making criteria matrix

Strategic opportunities	Match to core capabilities	Risk	Sales cycle	Align with vision
1. Grow value of existing clients (15% on last year's $9.9 million sales)	✓	Low	✓	✓
2. Develop new service range based on customer research feedback	✓	Low	✓	✓
3. Expand into Sydney via setting up local sales office	✓	Medium	Slower as design team in Melbourne	✓
4. Acquire a design company as entry to Sydney market	Yes – culture needs to be right	High	✓ Should be about the same	Yes
5. Expand into Sydney via existing sales team travelling to Sydney	✓	Low. Weakens Melbourne office	Longer sales cycle	Yes – as long as no impact on service
6. Set up online business to sell generic designs	✗	Low	To be confirmed	No
7. Acquire supply chain components to reduce costs	✗	Medium	✓	Maybe

This table can be downloaded from www.jennystilwell.com.au/sbceo/decisionframework

Stage 3 Action Plan – Business Expansion

Note: Table to be read across two pages

In plan period	Uses available	Existing business funds	Existing people model	Potential value plan period	Rank
✓	✓	✓	✓	$1.5 million	1
✓	✓	✓	✓	$500,000	2
✓	✓	✓	1 new	$300,000	3
✗	✗	Will need adjustments	No	High	More work to assess
✓	✓	✓	✓ Drain on existing people	$200,000?	3 is best option if we want market share
No	✓	No	Need new experts	To be confirmed	Low
Possible	✓ May need larger space	TBD	✗	Cost save; deliver faster	TBD

Table 8.11: Strategic Priorities – Summary Action Plan

Strategic focus in order of rank	Actions	Who	When
1. Build value of existing client base (15% on LY $9.9 million)	Bring in a sales coach to address weaknesses in sales processes immediately. 1. Set up sales processes and checklists to build customer relationships, develop strategic account plans, and identify new business opportunities. 2. Implement a customer management system around strategic classification of customers (tiers 1, 2, 3, 4). 3. Hold weekly sales meetings.	Jack Sam Jack Jack	15 March 20 April 28 February Start 1 February
2. Expansion into Sydney via setting up local rep office	Do P&L projections for Sydney business. 1. Recruit business development manager and set clear objectives for 6 months. 2. Provide induction training and client introductions to Sydney counterparts.	Susannah Susannah Susannah	End February End March End April
3. Develop new service range based on client feedback	Conduct client research. 1. Collate results and identify new service needs. 2. Develop service offering and value proposition. 3. Set up internal processes so we can deliver. 4. Test product, test existing client uptake, grow market share.	Mandy Mandy Mandy/Jemma Adam Adam	End March 15 April Mid-May End May
4. Expand core capabilities to reduce manufacturing costs and improve turnaround	Financial analysis of supply chain costs to assess potential efficiencies and competitive advantage. 1. Develop project plan to buy in and implement new machinery and equipment. 2. Assess space and fitout costs. 3. Look at leasing options.	Hugh Hugh/Tim Tim Hugh	Mid-March End April Mid-May End May

weekly basis. However, your team needs to know that a weekly meeting is not, by default, an opportunity to push out their deliverable date! Keeping this step simple is essential for execution.

Years ago I was brought in to one of the business units of a larger company with multiple business units. The parent company had just spent a million dollars with one of the top global consulting firms to do a complete review of their whole business. The review was incredibly detailed on every level, as you would expect. But the reason I was brought in by one of the business unit heads was because they needed me to interpret what the consulting firm had produced, and convert it into something that his team could actually understand and act on.

Don't underestimate the power of keeping it simple.

Chapter worksheets

- Strategic Planning Preplist™ – www.jennystilwell.com.au/sbceo/planpreplist
- Strategic Mini-Review – www.jennystilwell.com.au/sbceo/minireview
- Strategic SWOT Template – www.jennystilwell.com.au/sbceo/swot
- Decision-Making Framework – www.jennystilwell.com.au/sbceo/decisionframework

Find these worksheets and tools in the book's Companion Guide, which you can download here: www.jennystilwell.com.au/sbceo

Chapter highlights

- As the CEO you need to know and understand the numbers in your business. If you want to make the right decisions, and continue to strengthen your organisation, you can't escape the analysis.

- You need to take many strategic considerations into account so you make the best decision for where your organisation is positioned.

- Analyse what's really going on in your business using Strategic Planning Preplist™, Strategic Mini-Review and Strategic SWOT.

- Develop a framework for your business so you can make the right strategic decisions at the right time.

- Create a roadmap with strategies, actions, timeframes and accountabilities for everyone in your team to follow.

CHAPTER 9

Stage 4 – Optimise Value

BETTER business, better life! This is the stage when the owner of the organisation has decided to sell, and maximise their returns from usually many years of commitment to growing their business. Someone indicates interest, the business owner thinks of a figure that they'd be happy to sell for, and discussions proceed along that basis. Sometimes no agreement is reached, and the owner of the organisation goes back to their business. What should be happening at this stage – and actually well before it – is a strategic approach to how shareholder returns will be maximised when it's time to sell out.

Who is in Optimise Value stage?

- Any established business that has been through the expansion stage at least once and is attractive to external investors or acquirers (if you try and sell before this stage you won't be maximising value).
- Any organisation whose owner is ready to sell.

Challenges of Optimise Value stage

- Being prepared in advance if someone *approaches you* to buy your business.
- Shifting your focus from what your business *makes* to what it is *worth* – most business owners have no experience in selling a business so this process is unknown territory for them.

Being prepared in advance

The best way to be prepared is to start optimising your business back in the early stages of growth. Build the right structure, get the right people on board, set up the business to be able to run without you being there, and use strategic planning and reviews as a tool to drive your business forward.

Part of 'being prepared' is having given some consideration to what type of sale you may make, and what sort of companies may want to acquire you. Of the various options for selling your business, some will be more appropriate for you at the time, and some are more common.

Trade sale/business sale/strategic acquisition

An outright business sale is common for small- and medium-sized organisations, who typically sell to a larger company who can incorporate their people, equipment, brands and other intellectual property into their own existing business.

Not every acquirer will want to retain your existing team, so if you want to look after your team once you've sold, you need to establish this upfront.

Some acquirers may want your brands or your client base or some of your assets, but they may not want all the people or all the assets or all of the liability currently held by the business. They may or may not want the incumbent CEO or owner to stay on board as part of the handover process. In many cases, the existing owner may be asked to stay on board for a period of time to ensure that clients don't defect, and in particular that forecast sales come to fruition. It's an insurance policy for the acquirer, and payment for the organisation is often made in tranches on achievement of certain milestones during the handover.

When you are in Stage 4 it's definitely worthwhile to know what sort of terms you will and will not accept.

One business owner I know was offered a sum that was more than twice what he thought he would get for his business, but the acquirer was a multinational and wanted to keep him on board for three more years. They wanted him to stay as their rainmaker and report to someone else as part of the arrangement. He considered this offer, but realised that he hadn't built his business asset simply to sell out and effectively become a salaried salesperson for the next three years.

Management buy-out (MBO)

One or more managers within the business buy out the owners in a management buy-out. It is common for the acquirers to provide an initial payment or deposit to the owner. The benefits of this kind of sale are that it can be planned in advance and executed over a period of time, it is an easy option as business can continue as usual, the owner knows and trusts the people or person buying the organisation and the acquirers are familiar with the business they're acquiring. It also provides time to prepare the management team, or manager, to take over if that's required.

If the management team has been employing and building their team, and running the company on a day-to-day basis, it's unlikely that they will do anything too disruptive once they've acquired it. This may be a preferred option for the owner.

It is worth noting that in some cases, for both trade sales and management buy-outs, the acquirers don't have the necessary capital at the time to acquire the business in full. A finance option is often used where the owner of the organisation (vendor) finances the sale for the acquirers. This is called *vendor finance* – the vendor essentially agrees on a purchase price with the buyer, and then allows the buyer to pay the amount in instalments within a set period of time.

The buyer can take over the running of the organisation once the agreement has been signed, and start to focus on growth. The vendor is paid in instalments that the buyer funds from profits. In order to keep the buyer payments on track, an annual interest charge is usually applied, as an incentive for the buyer to pay off the 'loan' as fast as possible. This enables a buyer to acquire a business without having the full amount upfront, and enables the vendor to exit the business and continue to be paid out of the organisation's profits for the duration of the loan agreement.

Often an initial lump-sum payment will be required as part of this arrangement.

Merger

This is not really an exit strategy, certainly not in the immediate term. It's more of a stepping stone to selling your merged organisation for more than you would receive if you were to just go it alone.

As with many things, there can be a tendency for business owners to think more is better, or bigger is better. It isn't if you don't know what you're doing and you don't execute it strategically. Let's do some basic numbers.

Your company is turning over $10 million with a 10% net profit. Let's just assume the buyer values it at three times the profit and offers you $3 million.

Alternatively, you merge your organisation with another one just like yours, and with a few economies of scale, you make 15% net profit on $20 million turnover. A buyer offers you three times profit as the buy price and you and the owner of the company you merged with walk away with $4.5 million each. If you can leverage off your combined assets and grow the company to $30 million, making 15% net profit, that's a potential sale price of nearly $7 million each.

The reality is that the merger is less likely to go to plan when business owners have no experience in merging businesses together, and if they decide to merge without getting the right advice on whether it's actually a good strategy or not. Unlike when one company acquires another and removes a lot of duplicate roles and people and cost from the combined entity, a privately owned merged company tends to retain the most expensive people (the owners) and their associated costs.

Business owners are reluctant to let people go, which is understandable, but not financially viable when joining two companies together. Do you really need two office managers and two financial controllers (and two CEOs)? One of the benefits of merging is meant to be economies of scale.

And when you merge with an organisation that is located on the other side of town, there will be issues with location. Some people will leave if they add another 90 minutes to their commute each day. If the businesses both remain in their existing locations, the economies of scale are unlikely to happen to the extent they could if they were combined. Is there enough room to merge two businesses into one building or office? In that case, there are the costs of relocating plant and equipment and other assets.

The big thing to merge is the people – often different cultures, different ways of doing business, duplication of roles and people, deciding how to manage channels, customers and new products and services. These are all strategic considerations that are often not thought through prior to the merge, and will add costs into the new entity rather than strip them away.

The business owners have to focus on the challenges that will arise from merging. They will also need to be clear on their own roles, and know that certainly in the beginning most of the staff will continue to report to the person they're used to, whether that's the right person or not.

I know from experience that mergers can be done, and can be done well. I also know that many are not done well and do not represent the best option for growth, or exit, for the owners.

To finish on our sample numbers: we have merged two $10 million companies that previously did 10% net profit.

The merger wasn't handled well and they struggle to grow beyond their combined turnover of $20 million. They've incurred considerable operational expenses in making this transition – legal, financial, HR and team training among other costs – and with both founders still in the business the costs have not pared back much.

After the merger they do $20 million in sales and their net profit has dropped slightly to 9.5%. On a multiple of three times profit their potential sale price is $5.7 million. Half each and they walk away with $2.85 million, less than the $3 million they could potentially have sold out for had they not merged.

If they are able to pull themselves up from the upheaval of an unstructured merger and start to leverage off their combined assets to take business from their competitors and grow their combined customer base closer to $30 million in sales, the exercise will have been worth it. But they won't be able to exit until that point, in order to make the merger worth it. It could typically take another three to five years to grow the combined entity to $30 million or more.

Again, this is a simplified example to illustrate the pros and cons of private mergers.

Initial public offer (IPO)

An initial public offer is where you sell *part* of your company by making an offer to others to become shareholders. The business will then become a public company and the owner will be responsible to shareholders and a board in exchange for the funds acquired through the sale of shares. To many business owners this sounds like the sexy option because of the potential financial upside, raising millions through issuing shares. Sexy, maybe; hard work, definitely.

An IPO is not really an exit strategy, as you cannot typically sell all your shares to the public and depart the scene! Doing an IPO can be like platinum handcuffs. The contrast is incredibly confronting – from running your own show, unaccountable to anyone, to being accountable and answerable to shareholders, potential investors, business analysts, a board and the media.

It is rare for owners to do an IPO and exit at the same time. You will invariably be tied to your organisation to continue its growth and make sure certain objectives are achieved. If you should decide to sell any of your shares you will be accountable to all and sundry, including speculation by the media as to why you may be selling.

Would you like to read a piece in the daily media stating that you sold down a parcel of your shares to get your kids through their last two years of private schooling? Whichever way you try and explain it, it will never sound good.

You will be faced with a myriad of compliance requirements including Sarbanes-Oxley (legislation specifying accounting and reporting standards to protect investors from fraudulent activity) and ASIC; your management reporting will require a whole new level of rigour for the scrutiny of investors and analysts; and annual general meetings of shareholders are unlikely to become your favourite events – life in a fishbowl.

The other consideration with a public company is that the value of the shares is not always related to the actual growth or profitability of the business, but may lurch and dive off the back of what's happening in the stock market.

IPOs require a lot of work to prepare the company to go public. You need to start reporting like a public company, being compliant on all fronts with complete transparency, which is usually a higher level than most business owners have ever been used to; put your own board in place to set up the rigours of management reporting and accountability; and have the capital to pay for this exercise.

While you take your show on the road to brokers, analysts and investors you won't be focused on the day-to-day operations of your company, so you'd better have the right team in place. The actual cost of the capital raising could run into the millions. And after you've become a public company, there are the costs of being a public company.

Some of the costs incurred in going public are:

- legal advice – on the public offer; restructuring as a public company
- financial advice – on the public offer; reporting; compliance
- underwriting fees – by the merchant bank, as a percentage of capital raised
- preparation of information memorandum documents and supporting information
- external auditors
- set-up of agreements and incentive packages including share parcels for key employees

- set-up of an internal human resources function if it doesn't already exist in your company
- media relations (internal and/or external).

Once you have set up as a public company so you can sell off part of your shareholding to the public, you will then also incur ongoing costs of running a public company by way of infrastructure and compliance.

Most public companies are either:

- spin-offs from existing public companies
- new companies with potentially sizeable opportunities to take off in their market, e.g. high tech, biotech.

Because of the costs and investment involved in going public, it is generally not considered to be a good strategy unless your business is doing $20 million or more in revenue. After reading all of this, if you decide you want to go for the brass ring and give it your best shot, don't say I didn't warn you!

Shifting your focus to business value

When an acquirer is interested in your business, and you are interested in selling it to them, it will get down to a process of *due diligence*, whereby the potential purchaser of your business reviews all aspects of it before putting an offer on the table.

The more information you can access about your business the easier this process will be. For example, monthly management reports, client data, legal and other financial documents will all be required as part of the due diligence process. The more organised you and your company records are, the better.

The key challenge here is to not undersell your business. It's tempting to be excited about the big payoff after all your years of hard work, but if this is the reward you need to make sure it's as large as possible. Intellectual property makes up typically 75% and more of any organisation's assets, so turn your attention to the potential value it could provide your acquirer. IP includes things like brands, client databases, methodologies, trademarks and registered marks, software, client value and tenure.

Keys to success in Stage 4

- Have your business independently valued by someone who knows your industry, before you are ready to sell. This is not an essential key to success but it is a good way to help prepare you for this stage. Use the information you discover here to start optimising the value of your business. You may do this back in Stage 3.

- Be investor-ready. Have your information ready and at hand. The better prepared you are, the stronger your position for negotiation. No-one knows your business like you do.

- Get professional advice. I've seen business owners try to manage this process themselves and they have really done themselves a great disservice.

- Stay calm and make sure the acquirer is the right fit for your organisation. The better the fit, the more they will pay for your business. Remember, acquirers could potentially be based anywhere in the world, not just your local market. The process will take many months at least, so knowing that upfront will help with your game plan.

- Keep your own counsel. Do *not* share this with anyone you don't trust implicitly. If it gets out into the market it will weaken your position.

Optimise Value examples

RICHARD – FMCG BRAND COMPANY

Richard's company went through the classic Stage 2 challenges of fast growth, lack of structure and ad hoc expansion of the team without clear accountabilities, and in the early stages the managing director was loathe to let go. It operated in a dynamic and fast-moving market, and the company culture was the same – very fast-moving and responsive to new opportunities.

He took a lot of convincing, but when the company grew to the point where it was turning over sales revenue in the eight figures, the MD finally had the resources and definitely the need to structure the company with some seasoned senior managers. With these key executives basically managing the company, it left the MD free to focus on what he was so good at – creating new growth opportunities.

The new executives brought systems, management practices and reporting procedures to the business. Business systems were upgraded, financial reporting became detailed, accurate and regular, and monthly board meetings were held.

In addition to this, annual strategy sessions were held with the team to map out the strategic priorities and roadmap for the next 12 months. The MD's focus had shifted to building value into the company with a view to selling.

When the company eventually sold for $7 million it was the fruition of a long-held vision by Richard, who had focused on the value inherent in brands, which is what the acquirers wanted. Richard then had the opportunity to start a new venture. With lessons learned from the first venture, the second one sped through from Foundation to Business Expansion in a fraction of the time it took first time around.

Strategy is the key!

DAVID – MEDICAL PRODUCTS ORGANISATION

David was an entrepreneur intent on building a good organisation that would enable him to do business on a global scale and ultimately sell. Once he had transitioned through Stage 2 and his company was well established, he started to focus more on strategic growth and the future outcomes he wanted.

His initial strategy was to gradually put in place an experienced management team that could not only take over the day-to-day running of the business, but bring their own valuable ideas and experience into the organisation. He knew that he needed a good team to make his business grow further.

Detailed management reports were produced on a monthly basis and reviewed at their management meetings. He did his research into setting up an advisory board and started to recruit board members with a mix of skills and experience to benefit the business. This included board members with links into Asia – a destination market for them at the time – legal expertise, and experience within the relevant medical market.

He drew up Position Descriptions for his advisory board members which established what was expected of them in their roles. This company was leading the way in a growth market with niche products with increasing market demand. This was a primary driver of growth. From that point the company started to expand into Asia with controlled and deliberate growth strategies.

Approximately 10 years later the company was sold into a bigger public company entity. This was the perfect exit for David, but at the time he decided to stay on with a share in the larger global entity and play a significant role in continued growth.

He was able to sell his business because he had been focused on where he was taking it and what was required to get it there. He had market share, supply contracts, a strong team and board and a track record of executing on strategy.

Top 3 strategies to use in Stage 4

- Familiarise yourself with what acquirers look for and what they know, and where they see value in a business. What would make your business of most value and interest to them? Be prepared – you never know when someone will approach you about selling your company or other imperatives may dictate the timing of when you sell the business.

- Know what you want – why do you want to sell; what will you do next; are you ready to sell; do you want a big payday or a lifestyle income? Be honest about your answers. Either way you want to maximise your returns.

- Be investor-ready so you play this proactively. Make sure you've dealt with any deal-breakers, such as pending litigation or non-renewal of key contracts.

Chapter highlights

- You won't get the right price when you sell just because your company is strategic and profitable, if you don't know what you're doing through this process.

- It is essential to get sound advice to maximise your return.

- The earlier you start thinking about building value into your business and creating something of value that potential acquirers want, the better prepared you will be to optimise your returns.

CHAPTER 10

Stage 4 Action Plan – Optimise Value

TIME for rewards! Most business owners dream of this, but those who are expanding through Stage 3 start thinking seriously about optimising the value of their businesses. Nearly all of my clients have focused on growing their businesses so they can create a bigger future for themselves and the people they love. By the time you get to this stage, you need to be aware of some strategic considerations.

You need to know how to maximise the value of your organisation and what investors look for when assessing acquisition opportunities. It will also help if you know which types of organisations may be interested in your business, and why. The more strategic fit your business has to a potential acquirer, the more likely you will be valued at a higher multiple. The earlier you start thinking about these things the better.

Investors will look for a 'bargain' – an undervalued, underoptimised asset with potential for further growth. However, you want to optimise your value to make more when you sell. The sweet spot is where you have a valuable asset that has further potential for growth, that can only be realised with the particular resources that the investor brings to the table (refer to the Bobbi Brown example in Chapter 2, page 23).

We'll first look at what drives value, then at some guidelines as to how your business may be valued. And, finally, when you get to this point, I'd advise you against going it alone.

Why investors and acquirers buy

This checklist of what drives growth does vary between service and product businesses, with stock and capital equipment and other variables making the multiple calculations in particular quite different. The drivers listed here exclude factors which, although strategic, are out of your control, such as industry and market growth.

All of these drivers create value in your business, will make it function more efficiently and profitably, and will deliver more value to your clients now. So, why would other companies be interested in your business? These are the most common strategic reasons:

- **Access to a new geographic market** – for example, a Sydney company may acquire another company in Melbourne to gain quick access to the market; likewise international companies often use acquisition as their new market-entry strategy. Acquiring a company in an international market instantly puts you ahead in terms of local legal and financial knowledge, language and cultural awareness of the norms of doing business in that country.
- **Access to new market segments** – this would apply if your business specialised in one or more segments. For example, a general recruitment firm that has no legal practice may acquire a specialist legal recruitment firm.

Stage 4 Action Plan – Optimise Value

- **Access to technology and/or unique methodologies/IP/products and services** – easier to acquire than to develop, providing you have a track record with that technology or methodology (refer to the Case Study, page 217).
- **Speed** – acquisitions obviously enable growth to be achieved much faster. Many companies prefer to acquire numerous small businesses as a means of becoming a large company, as it's easier to integrate a small business into the existing business, and can be done faster than if you acquire one larger company. Scaling up fast may be a precursor to another strategy, such as sale or IPO.
- **Industry rollup** – some investors will consolidate an industry where there may be hundreds of small businesses each competing for a small percentage of market share and a few large players. In the 'rollup' they will acquire many of the small businesses, forming one large new company that has ready-made a major share of the market and economies of scale.
- **Access to your client base** – faster to acquire than grow organically; a client base that is compatible with the acquiring business will provide a new built-in market for the acquirer's existing products and services. If the acquired client base also has an associated annuity [ongoing] income, such as support fees, hosting fees, maintenance fees, or retainers, that is even better.
- **Acquirer removes you as a competitor** – can occur when you have a niche position/service/brand/technology/etc. that represents an obstacle to the acquirer competing for your business. In my experience this is a far less common reason for a small- or medium-sized organisation to acquire another.
- **Your business has distribution channels** that provide increased market access for the acquirer's products/services.

These channels may be online or offline, national or international, niche or mass market. If, for example, your business had a field sales force that serviced national pharmacy networks, your business may be attractive to a pharmaceutical or cosmetic company that wanted increased national distribution through pharmacies.

- **Brands** with high recognition and profitable, sustainable margins are attractive to acquirers, whether the brand is a service or a product. There are companies and investors that focus on acquiring stables of strong brands for both national and international markets. If you have strong brands – either your own, or exclusive distribution rights for a geographic region for someone else's brand, this will be attractive to the right investors and add considerable value to your business. If your organisation is in the business of selling and marketing brands, make sure they are your own, or contracted distribution rights with a third party success brand. Just look at all the companies who have built portfolios of brands through acquisition, such as Pacific Brands, LVMH, The Just Group, Pharmacare, and Capelle.

Some final considerations on value

Systems and processes for service delivery. The more your service delivery is based on processes, unique methodologies and approaches that are documented and trademarked where possible, the more you create value that is unique to your business. It creates a more consistent experience for your clients and service delivery is less individual-sensitive. Focus on what you do and how you deliver it, rather than who delivers it, to add more inherent value to your business. A service that can be delivered by new people/the acquirers/anyone but the people who developed it, is more valuable as it can be scaled up and evolved into other service offerings. If another firm with less advanced systems and processes than yours wants to acquire your

Stage 4 Action Plan – Optimise Value

business, they would want to take advantage of what you have created. This makes you more valuable to them. The same applies to product based companies, which typically have more complexity than service firms and are dependent on strong processes to deliver cost-effective products on time.

Client value and strong client relationships. This is important because it demonstrates your track record of acquiring and growing your clients over time. In order to do that, you need strong relationships and the ongoing development of relevant products and services that create fee multipliers. It will also be much easier to innovate with new products and services when you have the true insider perspective that strong client relationships provide. Building client value can, and should be, a system. Businesses are often acquired for their client base alone. If you have a client who is worth $10,000 a year and in three years' time is still worth $10,000 a year, then you win points for retention but nothing for client growth. An acquirer will look at the upside potential of a client base, to grow the overall value of different segments of clients. The value is not just the clients you've acquired, but what they could be worth if you systematically took a strategic approach to growth.

Strong distribution channels are highly sought after by product-rich companies. Even if your organisation has distribution channels in your own geographic market only, this will be extremely valuable to a product supplier wanting to gain entry to your market. If you had a sales force that reached GPs and medical clinics, this would be highly valuable to a supplier of pharmaceutical or medical products. If you had a network of computer resellers across the country, that would be highly attractive to a vendor of compatible hardware products. If your business is an online model and you have a network of affiliates, that channel would be attractive to an acquirer wanting to expand their sales of related products or services online.

A track record of top and bottom line performance. Don't be fooled by forecasts. Potential acquirers often get extremely excited about the potential upside of an acquisition, based on the company's forecasts for the future. Make sure your sales forecasts and projected P&L forecasts can be explained. You need to be able to explain the assumptions they're based on, previous performance or results, and identify known revenue compared with speculative revenue. If you have a good handle on this, plus previous results from previous years, your forecasts will be more robust and a more accurate indicator of future revenue streams for an acquirer. I've seen forecasts made out of nothing but hope, which fall apart with a few probing questions. A track record and a sound understanding of where your sales come from and why, is the strongest indicator of future potential performance. Be prepared.

When we talk about multiples you'll see that growth in both sales revenue and profitability *can be* crucial elements in driving a high value for your service business. If you have a good track record of performance growth you will be able to bargain for a higher sale price for your business. However, there are companies that may have an enviable customer base that they don't service well, or don't have any new products to offer to that customer base, that will be under-valued because they haven't maximised that potential. Acquirers find these sorts of undercapitalised opportunities very attractive, but you don't want to be an undercapitalised bargain!

The Business Analyst Question™

Some years ago, as CEO of a company I ran at the time, I was giving a presentation to a room full of business analysts from stockbroking firms. Near the end of the presentation, one of the analysts asked me 'How do you make money?' He wanted me to go back and explain that again. I thought he was mad or had fallen

Stage 4 Action Plan – Optimise Value

asleep somewhere along the way, but there was method to his apparent 'madness'. In spite of what I'd already said, he wanted me to take him through the process and explain exactly, step by step, how we 'did what we did' in delivering a range of products and services to our customers. As I discovered, his objective was to assess whether we were maximising all of our potential revenue opportunities.

It was an interesting way of looking at the business model, and one I have used ever since. Value, and profit, is built into your business model at the points at which you can, and could, deliver value and service to your clients, and ultimately make money.

So the real question is: 'How and *where* do you make money?'

Map out your process for how you deliver your product or service and how you follow up. Identify whether you are 'leaving any money on the table'. For example, if your primary product is custom-developed business to business software applications, you generate revenue from sales of the product, probably on a per user licence fee basis.

Depending on how you deliver your product and service, and the type and size of your client base, you could also be making money from:

- support – ad hoc, or for specified periods
- training – user
- training – administrator
- training – train the trainer
- training – refresher
- software upgrades and new modules
- training – on new upgrades
- maintenance – ad hoc, and annual fees
- customisation – reports
- hardware sales

- hardware upgrades
- software sales – other applications
- development
- offering up-sells to more feature-rich versions
- consulting – integration of systems.

Optimise multiples

Essential information you need to know about *multiples*:

- Business values are based on multiples, which is typically a multiple of revenue or profit.
- For private companies, the owners will usually take as much salary from the business as possible. This results in smaller profit and naturally a correspondingly lower company tax bill. In many cases, if a business is acquired and merged into a bigger entity, a CEO won't be required as there will already be one in the bigger business. For example, let's assume the business being sold shows a net profit before tax of $700,000 and pays the owner $500,000 in salary (and there will be other expenses that the business pays for the owner). Once that owner is no longer in the business that half million dollars will go to the bottom line. The real profit level will be $1.2 million. So, sometimes private company multiples are based on multiples of sales rather than profit, as true profit is distorted by owner expenses and salary.
- In *general*, a multiple on sales revenue is not unlikely in the range of 1 to 1.5 times revenue.
- Averages vary between industries, but services and consulting firms can be more attractive to some investors as there's no requirement to reinvest profit into things like plant, equipment and stock.
- If you focus on the drivers of value listed in this chapter, and on the strategies outlined in this book, your business

Stage 4 Action Plan – Optimise Value

performance, and therefore multiple, is more likely to result in a premium value for your business.

- A general rule of thumb for an EBIT multiple is between 1.5 to 3 times EBIT (earnings/profit before interest and tax), however, for the organisation producing outstanding results, that is highly attractive to a particular acquirer, a multiple of many times more could potentially be achievable *in the right market*.
- Multiples vary but are dependent primarily on the value drivers above producing consistent and predictable results. The better the business at having all the drivers in place, the more predictable will the revenue and EBIT be. That's attractive to investors.

Note: Having said all of this, it all depends on the company being sold and its inherent value, for *whatever reason*, to the acquirer.

Here is a real-life case study to put some of the drivers into perspective:

Case study example

SOFTWARE COMPANY IN A NICHE SECTOR

- Been operating for 20-plus years
- Turnover $3 million
- EBIT 13% ($400,000)
- Founders/owners still operational in business and won't let go
- External GM appointed
- Approximately 40 staff (*Note:* $75,000 revenue per head is low for a software company, which indicates that the headcount is way too high relative to sales volume)
- No real barriers to entry – an organisation could potentially set up distribution of a competitive product quite quickly
- Estimated cost to develop similar software from the ground up is $5 million
- The company has branches in five states of Australia

- 40% of annual income is annuity revenue
- Revenue streams: software; support; training
- Leadership position in its market sector
- Its niche is a growth sector but there are many competitors globally
- Revenue projections by the GM indicate 240% growth in 3 years (it's taken 20 years to reach $3 million; is another $7 million in three years feasible?).

Assessment

- The business could raise capital for growth through private equity, but the founders would have to go.
- The founders could sell the business outright in a trade sale.
- On a multiple of earnings the value of the business has been estimated at 4 to 5 times – $2 million ($400,000 EBIT x 4 or 5).
- Or, based on the IP value, this business at the time was estimated to have a sale value of around $5 million (the cost to reproduce the software from scratch).
- The latter would be the best option, of course, and the value is obviously not based on a sales or profit multiple.
- There are many strategic and financial considerations when buying and selling companies. Think strategically if you want to maximise the potential value of your business, and understand your market and your real opportunities.

Don't go it alone

You've come this far – now is *not* the time to wing it and sell your business by yourself. You need advice, support and an expert who can help you navigate this stage. Here are my two top pieces of advice to help you find and work with the expert advisors you need.

Stage 4 Action Plan – Optimise Value

Employ a corporate advisory firm

They will handle the sale of your business while you keep focused on your day-to-day business. They can put together the necessary documents to help sell your company, which effectively becomes your marketing campaign. They will put together an initial summary of highlights about your business, as a preliminary document to generate interest in the market.

They can contact companies and investors who may be interested in you, and maintain confidentiality within your market. The last thing you want is an industry rumour going around that you are trying to sell your company.

When investors are genuinely interested in assessing your business, they will want an IM – an information memorandum. This is like a sexy business plan with images and highlights of your past performance, plus future plans and projections and sound reasons why your business would be a good investment. Your corporate advisory firm will put this together for you.

If they are the right firm for you, they will have access to private investors and venture capitalists both here and overseas, and can extend their net of potential acquirers way further than you ever could. They will handle all communication and liaison until you are ready to meet with any potential acquirers.

Corporate advisory firms all have different fee structures and how they deliver their services to you. What is most important is whether they can get an outcome that you want. These factors are important when choosing who you will work with:

- Do they have experience in your industry? If so, they should understand your business model and inherent value to potential acquirers.
- What is their process, expected timeframe, and fees?
- What is their track record? They should be able to demonstrate with similar case studies to yours.

- What are their credentials, reputation and results? Ask around if you can – if you're part of a CEO group, you should be able to have this discussion confidentially with your peers. Ask for references from owners of companies that they have sold successfully.
- Who will be handling your sale? Your initial meeting may be with a partner of the firm, but the bulk of the project may be run by junior consultants.
- Do you have rapport with the team who will be looking after you? Selling your business can be a stressful and emotional time, and you need to trust and be comfortable with the people handling it.

Know what you want

Throughout this process, the corporate advisory firm will ask you questions, but may just present different scenarios instead. For example, they may tell you that they have a private equity firm interested in buying your business, if you stay on as CEO and help build it further over the next two years. You may not have voiced what you want at this point, but it's important to know upfront as it will help clarify the process for everyone.

Here are some considerations:

- Who may want to acquire you?
- What sort of companies in this industry could be likely acquirers?
- What about international companies – how would you feel about a company based in India, China, the US or elsewhere acquiring your business?
- Would you be prepared to stay on as CEO?
- How long would you be prepared to stay on for?
- Are you prepared to sign a non-compete agreement for 12/24/36 months?

Stage 4 Action Plan – Optimise Value

- What about your team? How well do you want to look after them? Is that important to you?
- When are you going to tell them about this?
- How are you going to handle that discussion and the exit process with your team?

A client of mine refused to get advice for this stage, and preferred instead to go it alone. He was offered an indicative price by a much larger company that wanted a larger slice of market share. My client was excited – possibly blindsided by – the price they were talking, but the offer was to tie him to the company for another two years as the sales and marketing director.

After growing and running his own business for 30 years, he was being asked to step aside and look after sales and account management, and let someone else run the company and make strategic decisions. He would be on a salary with tranches of the purchase price being paid on achievement of certain targets.

Would you have accepted that offer? He didn't either.

Another client of mine sold his business, following the steps outlined in this process. He was also offered a similar arrangement by one prospective buyer, who wanted to retain him to run the company and grow it further. Because of the process we'd been through to prepare him for this stage, he knew upfront the terms he wouldn't accept and what he wanted to achieve financially and personally. He achieved what he wanted – with another buyer.

Being clear about what you want, getting the right advice, and letting someone handle your negotiations if you're not used to it – these will all contribute to you optimising the value of your business and walking away with your big payday.

Chapter highlights

- Before you start the process to sell your business, it will be to your advantage if you understand what investors and acquirers look for when buying a business.
- You also need to think about what it is that you will and won't accept with the terms your acquirers ask.
- Get professionals to help you through the process.

CHAPTER 11

Staying on Track

IT'S important to manage your business and track and monitor growth. Every successful business has a system to focus on priorities. There are many ways to keep yourself on track, whether we're talking about a business strategy, a fitness program, a set of personal goals, or anything at all that we want to achieve. When it comes to executing your business strategy, these are the simplest and best methods that work for me, and all my clients.

Big rocks – the power of focus

Imagine you have some big rocks, some pebbles, some sand, some water and a large glass jar. First, put all your big rocks into the jar. There will be gaps around those rocks, so you'll have room for the small pebbles. You could fit a bit more in that jar, so you fill up the extra space with sand. Finally, you could add water to fill in any last little gaps and crevices of air. Now, try to do that in reverse.

In *The 7 Habits of Highly Effective People*, Stephen Covey wrote about big rocks. In a nutshell, if you don't get the big rocks in first, you'll never fit them in. The big rocks are your major projects or activities that will move your business forward. They aren't your to-do list; they are actions that align with your strategy and, once complete, will result in your business moving closer toward the vision you have created for it.

As you work through the strategic priorities for the stage of growth your business is currently in and create a strategic roadmap for your business, make sure you highlight the big rocks.

For example, if updating your website is important, but not something that will help you sell more or make more money this month, then it isn't a big rock. If updating your website means you will be able to add the shopping cart and finally upload the three products you have to sell, and can then start promoting to your customer base, then that *is* a big rock.

Finding the right corporate advisory firm to sell your business is definitely a big rock when the time is right. If it helps you make money, save money, saves you time, or ultimately helps you grow in some way, it is probably a big rock.

Management reporting

Make sure you get, and use, timely and accurate management reports. You need to be able to track the key indicators in your business – not just sales revenue, but other important indicators that will vary with different business models, but may include:

- sales per day/week/month
- sales by product/service
- new clients per week/month
- average value per client
- customer churn
- return on your marketing activities – results
- percentage of expenses to sales
- net new subscribers per week/month

- average online sales value
- margin by product or brand or service
- sales by salesperson per week or month
- number of units of product made and ordered
- total invoice value per week or month
- sales revenue per square metre of retail space
- actual sales vs forecast
- client feedback – testimonials, general feedback, problems
- number of service errors or problems logged
- number of service errors or problems resolved
- speed of service problem resolution
- revenue per employee
- profit per employee
- average value per project/transaction
- media coverage per month
- average sales transaction size per day/week.

If you don't know what the right indicators and reports are for your business, start with the basics like sales, margin, profit, units sold and new customers, and use this list to test other indicators that could apply in your business. Management reports and dashboards may be charts, graphs, words, numbers or infographics or any combination that works best for you. These are just a few systems to keep you focused on the priorities that will make your business a more valuable asset now, and in the future.

Accountability

At an individual employee level, performance reviews are designed to keep everyone in your company on track and accountable. Regular structured meetings with a clear and brief agenda help everyone to stay on top of need-to-know information and activities. Meetings produce the best results when attendees know beforehand what the agenda will be, what they are expected to contribute, what they need to bring or report on, and how long it will run for. Always walk away from a meeting knowing that it achieved its purpose.

If you want to succeed, make yourself accountable. Make your team accountable. We all perform to much higher levels if we are held accountable to other people. You could use any or all of these options:

- One-on-one meetings with you on a weekly, fortnightly or monthly basis.
- Regular internal team meetings where everyone is held accountable to follow through on their allocated areas of responsibility.
- Quarterly review meetings with your team – either your own team or your virtual team of service providers – to stay on track with quarterly or 12-monthly goals.
- Operations reviews with larger teams on a quarterly or six-monthly basis to track execution of strategy against the annual plan. They provide an opportunity to address any problems or new opportunities, and course-correct accordingly. They also keep everyone accountable.
- Strategic retreats annually with your team are essential for taking time out to think and plan for the next 12 months.
- Board meetings – if you have a board of directors, or even an advisory board, make sure you have regular meetings at which you take and distribute the minutes. It's good corporate governance and evidence of a company that follows good management practices. Don't forget to make your board accountable to achieve its key results for the company.

Set yourself up for success

Take your business down the strategic path of your choice because it's what you really want to do. Don't just choose a strategy and pursue an opportunity because you *can*. If you have a disconnect between what you really want and what you think you should do, your heart will obey and you won't follow the strategy outlined for your business. Set yourself up for success by aligning your life vision with your business vision.

Use these tools to keep you focused on priorities, to guide you and keep you moving toward what you want for yourself and the big picture of your life.

Revisit your growth potential – products, client base and channels in particular – frequently and don't neglect these key business fundamentals. Don't neglect your team, and try to spend time thinking about leverage and innovation, and how it could lift your business to a whole new level of operation. Above all, do it because you love it and because it gives you fulfilment and enjoyment.

I wish you success and happiness in your creation of an inspiring and exciting bigger future!

Chapter highlights

- Remember to get the big rocks in first as they are the things that will move your business forward.

- One-on-ones with key people in your team are a fundamental way to keep across the priorities in your business, and keep your key people focused on the same thing. I recommend you do them weekly.

- Set yourself up for success by tracking your priorities, measuring results against forecasts and plans, and making your team accountable.

- Know your numbers. What are the most important numbers to track that will really measure the progress of your business? Take the time to identify what these are – it will make a real difference.

Acknowledgements

There are many people to thank, who have encouraged and supported me in the journey of giving birth to my first book.

I am fortunate to have worked with some wonderful colleagues and clients. Through different means they have all provided me with insights and experiences that in some way have contributed to the content of this book.

I would like to give special thanks to my clients in stages two and three, many of whom have remained on this journey alongside me for many years. I am extremely grateful for having such a wonderful opportunity to work with these amazing people who allowed me in to their businesses to work with their teams, helping them create better, stronger companies.

I would like to thank my assistant Natalie Barnes, who reignited my enthusiasm and motivation with energetic cheerleading and highly intelligent ideas and input. She definitely made this book better than it was before her contribution!

Finally, and most importantly, I have to thank my family for unfailing and unconditional love, support and belief in me always.

About Jenny Stilwell

Jenny Stilwell is a business advisor, consultant, speaker and author of Small Business CEO. For the better part of the last 20 years, Jenny has made a career of running businesses – both her own and others' – and advising clients how to create stronger companies. She is a specialist in creating the right structure and strategy for business growth. Since founding her mentoring consultancy in 2002, she has been providing advice for CEOs of small and medium sized companies on using better strategies to create better businesses.

Prior to that Jenny was one of only very few females in Australia at the time to head up a publicly listed company, first as CEO then as Managing Director on the board.

She has two Bachelor Degrees from the University of Melbourne, is a Certified NLP Practitioner, has been a Finalist in the Telstra Business Women's Awards, has been interviewed for Qantas Business Radio twice and published in numerous business magazines. She is also a Graduate of the Australian Institute of Company Directors.

Jenny has presented learning content to CEO groups, run her own mastermind groups for small business CEOs, been Chair of

Marketing Women (Vic.) and also a mentor to women in the marketing profession as part of this program.

Jenny's unusual combination of corporate credentials at a senior executive and CEO level, combined with her experience in setting up and growing two professional consultancy practices of her own, make her extremely well qualified to talk and write about managing business growth.

In her spare time, she always has a writing project on the go, is working on reducing her golf handicap, loves chilling at the beach for weekends, travelling to new places and enjoys walking her beautiful Golden Retriever, Wiggie.

Jenny can be contacted at jenny@jennystilwell.com.au.

Other resources

Jenny's website has a range of resources covering business growth, management and strategy. There is a vast selection to choose from including blog articles and a list of recommended reading, as well as templates, checklists and workbooks from this book that you can download to work through in your own time. To get access to your free information, go to:

www.jennystilwell.com.au.

www.ingramcontent.com/pod-product-compliance
Ingram Content Group UK Ltd.
Pitfield, Milton Keynes, MK11 3LW, UK
UKHW021302180426
11947UKWH00015B/971